RISK
STARTS
AND
ENDS
WITH
people

Demystifying risk for executives and leaders

LISA SISSON

R^ethink

First published in Great Britain in 2021
by Rethink Press (www.rethinkpress.com)

Contents

For every leader who believes in the
power of people to create a better world

Foreword

I have a real passion for the subject of this book and have devoted most of my career to managing complex risks. In 1998, I co-founded a company, Digital Sandbox, that set out to build artificial intelligence algorithms to reason about low-probability, high-consequence risks, like terrorism, insider threats, geopolitical unrest and other hard-to-predict events. I was awarded several patents and our algorithms were used to allocate almost $20 billion in risk-based investments, as well as to guide the operational planning and risk management of events like the NFL's Super Bowl. As I write this, I've recently started a new company, Next5, to identify the critical emerging technologies of the next five years and to ensure that companies and governments are anticipating and planning for risk.

Beyond the analytical methods I've developed, in my personal and professional life I'm a risk-taker! I love change, adventure, building something from scratch, trying something for the first time, taking the path less travelled. But I don't do those things foolishly or recklessly – I live by rules of thumb and leverage frameworks, and I run risk models in my head all the time. On my leadership teams, I've come to learn that some are scared of change, some avoid risks, and some take unnecessary risks without having thought of the implications. In life, we all interpret the facts differently, we have different goals and objectives, we have different mental models. In our work lives, harnessing our different perspectives, developing an organisation and culture that excels at taking risks, and building the awareness and responsiveness to risk drivers allows us to accomplish great things, out-perform overly structured and risk-averse cultures, and be ready to adapt and adjust when we hit unex-pected obstacles.

I met Lisa in 2013 and, after some mutual due dili-gence, Digital Sandbox and Unearth became business partners. But, more than that, we became friends. We learned together and from each other, and we have continued along our journey to support each other. With a whole world between us, most of our conver-sations have been over email and on the phone (and more recently Zoom) but I've had the chance to travel in Australia with Lisa and her family a couple of times and she's spent time in the States with my company and family as well.

I won't forget my first trip to Australia – we had entered an innovation challenge together in Queensland, and since it was highly competitive, we couldn't make travel arrangements until we were chosen to compete. When we found out we'd been selected, I had little time to get to Australia, leaving me with a middle seat in the back of coach and twenty-four hours in the air. I landed to meet Lisa and John Sisson for the first time, groggy and bleary-eyed. Over the next few days, we learned, designed, worked hard and competed together – not ultimately 'winning' – but establishing a firm foundation for a relationship that lasts to this day. Perhaps we won after all. Relationships and partnerships like ours form the basis of who Lisa is and what she encourages in this book.

Over the years, we did business together in banks and in government, always seeking to help our customers understand and manage complex risks. This book reflects many of the lessons learned along the way. Lisa wisely focuses on people – not algorithms, as in my career – but rather the realisation that people, when properly managed and empowered, will help protect the enterprise from risks and find opportunities for growth. Alternatively, in a rigid structure of rules, reporting and penalties, organisations become slaves to the numbers, people are afraid to come forward, and risks can be buried, only to surface in negative outcomes.

In this past year or so, the world has felt the extraordinary power that threats and hazards can have on countries, companies and families. From pandemics to wild fires, and economic and trade disruptions to political change, we've been affected in extraordinary ways. This book provides practical advice on how to anticipate these threats, develop risk management programs, communicate with our extended teams, and ultimately protect our most valuable assets. I'm so grateful to Lisa for sharing part of her journey with me these past years, and now the insights and guidance in this book, which you can put into practice in your organisation and your life.

Bryan Ware
Founder and CEO of Next5, former Assistant Director of Cybersecurity and Infrastructure Security Agency (CISA)

Introduction

No organisation can afford to ignore risk. Whether it comes from environmental threats such as floods and fires, human threats such as terrorist attacks or computer viruses, or health threats such as an unexpected global pandemic, we must all plan for the possibility of things going wrong.

But the thing about planning for risk is that it can make us fixate on potential threats. We can become so worried about the things that might happen that we introduce systems of protection that are themselves sources of risk. We set up processes that slow down our businesses, frustrate our employees and create a culture of suspicion and mistrust, and these can cause more harm than the original threats we hoped to protect ourselves against.

In *Risk Starts and Ends with People,* you will be presented with a new perspective on risk. You will be shown how to protect yourself more effectively from potential threats, while at the same time creating a workplace culture that is supportive, transparent and resilient.

The vital importance of getting risk right means that it is also the source of a huge amount of anxiety, and even fear, for those tasked with managing it. Getting risk management wrong can mean the destruction of the organisation's assets – or its reputation. It can lead to harm being caused to employees or customers, including physical, psychological and emotional damage. For those decision-makers responsible for risk management, getting it wrong can also cause damage to personal reputations, which can end careers.

It's because of these high stakes that emotional, reactive and downright dangerous decisions are common in risk management. Risk has generated a multi-billion-dollar risk management industry, but all too often this industry trades on smoke and mirrors, selling concerned decision-makers solutions that are not adequately explained or customised or, worse, exaggerating threats to encourage leaders to make decisions out of fear.

We have seen this first-hand when working with companies who find themselves lost in a labyrinth of confusing risk management solutions. We've seen it when complex technology they have heavily invested in has been unsuccessful in identifying the range or depth of threats expected, often generating more noise and anxiety than useful information. We've seen it when a toxic work environment means that managers don't trust their own teams, or that employees don't trust the organisation. Many organisations that have addressed risk through tick-box or band-aid, bare minimum solutions have realised that a more holistic, granular and responsive approach is needed.

In this book, you will be introduced to a unique approach that has been highly effective for organisations fixated on risk. Workplaces unravelled by fear, suspicion, disengagement or malice can create the safety to drive transformational outcomes, mitigate risk, open up opportunities and empower their people, free from the fear of failure.

The secret? People.

People are at the very centre of risk, which is why risk starts and ends with people.

You'll come to understand just how powerful this simple statement can be. It will reorient everything you know about risk and give you a sudden and clear view of how risk develops inside an organisation and, crucially, how you can turn it around. You will be introduced to a comprehensive, tried-and-tested framework to 'protect the house' – *your* house. And you'll learn how to create a Safe Zone, within which you can harness your greatest asset – your people.

Time and time again, we've seen people apply these principles in their workplace to understand the vicious cycle causing them so much anxiety, so much tension, and so much risk. It is like an epiphany – the scales fall from their eyes and they gain clarity about the way people contribute to *and* protect against their organisational risk.

Risk Starts and Ends with People is written for CEOs and executives driven by a desire to create meaningful change. It's for the true leaders who are rolling up their sleeves to do the work that matters.

This book is a practical guide to leaving behind the fear and anxiety associated with risk. It is a toolkit for inspiring your people to become your risk sensors and to identify risk before it has the chance to inflict serious harm. It's a manual for creating a workplace where people are motivated to come to work, contribute their skills, innovate, problem-solve and push for excellence.

So come on, let's get started.

PART ONE
WHAT IS RISK?

1
Demystifying Risk

Most people see risk as equivalent to threat, hazard or harm. Risk feels a lot like danger – either physical or emotional – which could impact you personally or the things you care about, like your family, your home or your business. Many think of risk as something with negative consequences and, naturally, this makes people uncomfortable.

This is a normal and instinctive reaction. But risk and threat are not the same thing. As soon as you understand the difference, you can move towards a deeper understanding of how to manage risk.

In this chapter, we will take a close look at our natural physiological reactions to danger and threat. We'll examine the ways that we humans try to avoid dangers and threats by controlling our environment – that is, by assessing and controlling risks. Finally, we'll look at the multibillion-dollar risk industry and its culture of ambiguous language and confusing formulas which, to the less informed, can be no more than white noise. At best, this results in poor business decisions; and at worst, a false sense of security and ignorance of actual risk.

The Three Fs

It's completely natural to be disturbed by threats. If something threatens you, it triggers an automatic physiological reaction. This starts with concern or discomfort, and can progress to anxiety for some people or absolute fear and panic for others.

These reactions can be instinctive and beyond our conscious control. All living beings naturally desire to survive and flourish, which means that when faced with a threat, our primitive minds respond in one of three ways: fight, flight or freeze – aka the Three Fs.

The flight or fight response, also called the acute stress response, was first described by Walter Cannon in the 1920s. It postulated that animals react to threats with a general discharge of the sympathetic nervous system.[1] It was later expanded to include the freeze response, where we feel paralysed, unable to make a decision.

The moment we are confronted with something that makes us feel vulnerable, where we believe there is threat or potential harm, we move towards one of the Three Fs. If we equate risk to threat, it's no wonder we feel disturbed when thinking about risk, because our fight–flight–freeze response is activated.

Threat vs risk

Threats are things or people likely to cause damage or danger. Naturally, they cause uncomfortable feelings. When you are engaging in risk management, one of your objectives is to identify vulnerabilities that could be exploited by a threat (accidentally or intentionally). Exploring the potential threats and determining any vulnerabilities that make you susceptible to those threats is critical.

Sometimes it is not until an incident occurs that you find a threat that was not identified. Take Microsoft in 2021 for example – one moment, they were rewarding a bug bounty hunter for identifying and notifying them of a security vulnerability,[2] and just days later, they were the victim of a sophisticated attack that claimed at least 60,000 known victims globally.[3] Microsoft have their own internal testing and quality assurance process, but in certain industries, even with testing for Quality Assurance, vulnerabilities can be missed.

Microsoft are certainly not alone – there are many examples of organisations becoming aware of an unidentified vulnerability as a result of an incident or carried-out threat. Many organisations have found out the hard way, meaning that they had not anticipated or prepared for the scenario, leading to the damage, destruction or loss of the asset they were trying to protect.

Risk, on the other hand, refers to the potential for harm, loss or damage. It takes threats and vulnerabilities into account but also the value we place on an asset (the 'exposure').

Assets, threats and vulnerabilities can be understood as follows:

- **An asset** is a person, place or thing. Assets (things) can be tangible, like a computer, or intangible, like the data on that computer.

- **A threat** is an event likely to cause harm through damage, injury or pain – eg a storm, fire, flood or cyber-attack. Threat is sometimes referred to as the 'hazard'.

- **A vulnerability** is an environmental, genetic or physical factor that increases the likelihood of exposure to harm or attack. A person with a heart condition, or family history of such, is more vulnerable to heart attack than someone with no heart issues. A building in close proximity to the bush is more vulnerable to bushfire than one in the city. A business with poor security is more vulnerable to theft than one with more robust measures in place.

Risk is a calculation of these three factors that we can use proactively. It allows us to make an assessment prior to an actual threat arising, which is the point. Though we are often forced to make risk assessments under duress, we can also make them ahead of time, when we are not under pressure (under 'blue skies').

Calculating risk

There are different equations and standards that analyse risk. For example, the International Organization for Standardization (ISO) is an international organisation that develops standards to ensure quality, safety and efficiency of products, services and systems. The ISO standard 31000:2018 *Risk Management – Guidelines* looks at risk through the risk sources, potential events, their consequences and their likelihood.[4] A formula that seeks to simplify the concept is:

Asset × Threat × Vulnerability = Risk

In practice, you would say:

The value of the asset × The probability of the threat × The degree to which the asset is vulnerable = The level of risk

Assets can have supporting and complementary assets and their value can be aggregated. For example, organisations have buildings, servers, intellectual property, etc. Your organisation may stack-rank assets by the probability of the threat, the degree to which the asset is vulnerable to loss and the impact of such a loss, eg financial damage. This allows organisations to make informed decisions, including whether some types of losses are acceptable (eg legal liability, property loss, financial loss, or potential loss of customers or employees). This is why risk formulas often include:

- Exposure – the measure of the potential loss (or losses) that can be incurred as a result of the event.

- Consequences – the environmental impact of the event.

- Countermeasures (or measures) – your risk management response, which could incorporate a management system standard (eg ISO), process or similar to address the threats and vulnerabilities identified.

Determining the value of an asset requires context – for example, knowledge of its importance, worth or usefulness to a specific person or group of people, community or organisation. Sometimes damage to even a small or simple asset can bring an organisation unstuck.

The calculation allows people to make more informed decisions and look at ways to control the risk, according to their resources (eg money, people, assets and environment). Let's look at an example.

Imagine a national park (asset) in an area that often suffers from bushfires (threat). Inside the park are a number of telecommunication towers (assets) which provide critical communications to communities (exposure) and can be links for firefighters whenever there is a fire in the park. It's important to protect the towers because the fire could cut communications (risk).

To protect the national park (asset), the authorities regularly reduce the fuel load (vulnerability) inside the national park so fire (threat) intensity can be lessened to reduce the likelihood of it getting out of control (increased threat). To reduce the threat of fire to the telecommunication towers, they are constructed in less exposed areas, and the areas around the towers are kept clear of vegetation. However, the towers need to be on top of hills, and as fire travels fastest uphill there will always be some level of exposure and therefore residual risk.

There are many ways to view this example and the extent of the risk depends on how you value the communications capability. Whose viewpoint do you take?

Through the eyes of the emergency responders, communications may be critical to delivering response services, therefore ultimately this represents the safety of themselves and the community. From the telecommunications company viewpoint, the risk may be a commercial risk with loss of revenue or reputation, and the cost of reconstruction if seen not to do enough to protect the community. National Park Agencies may focus on the value and protection of their asset, the actual communications tower.

From the community perspective the loss of warnings, family contact, news, banking, internet and phones will all cause short- to long-term consequences. There may also be impact across a number of social, economic, health, supply and safety perspectives. All will be deeply personal to the individuals concerned.

Regardless of which viewpoint is taken, the community (people) is the common factor. While the different stances influence how we assess and determine risk, the compounding and confounding factors are essential to identify and consider when identifying the true risk. The challenge in situations like this is to identify just how many viewpoints there can be to determine the true risk:

Asset (Community, National Park and Communication Towers) × Threat (Fire) × Vulnerability (Fuel Load) = Risk (multiple potential risks to the community, including isolation, loss of communication, fire status, etc)

Risk management is about planning, reducing vulnerabilities and controlling the environment to reduce the chances of danger or harm. It's about understanding the importance of an asset, looking at the potential vulnerabilities, and then looking at potential threats to determine the risk. In this example, what would be the consequence of the telecommunication tower going down? Emergency responders could not respond to the fire as effectively with limited or no communications, and it may cut communications to people in the valley – they might not be able to make phone calls, or receive information to evacuate. These factors increase the value of the communications towers and would prompt increased planning around managing the risk to them as a priority. There may not be the same level of concern around lesser-value structures, such as park benches or play equipment.

Understanding your risk and appropriately responding is critical, especially if you work in a sector involving higher-risk environments. Examples include emergency response (eg law enforcement, fire, ambulance), defence and national security, political, legal, critical infrastructure, finance, insurance and superannuation, prisons and aged care.

We all make risk assessments and look to manage the risk in our lives. A practical example closer to home is how we buy insurance – we'll purchase it for our cars and homes, but not often for our bicycles. We can accept the loss of that asset, though we may still buy a bicycle lock to manage the potential risk of loss. In general, in our personal lives, we pay money and take simple actions every day to manage risk based on what we value and what we think is likely to happen to us.

The human advantage

Threats apply to all living beings. It doesn't matter whether you're an animal or a plant, a virus or bacteria. But humans are unique in leveraging additional data to calculate risk. Some would say this is due to our so-called 'higher intelligence', which we can apply to solve problems and head off threats. Or it could come from our need to control events, leading us to become fixated on our desired outcome and look for ways to be best equipped to make it happen.

Human intelligence is marked by complex cognitive feats and high levels of motivation and self-awareness. Humans possess the cognitive abilities to learn, form concepts, understand, apply logic and reason. Our intellectual capacity includes the abilities to recognise patterns, plan, innovate, solve problems, make decisions, retain information and use language to communicate.

As humans have evolved, we have found creative ways to protect ourselves from different types of threats. We have grown beyond the basic need to safeguard our food, build shelter to protect ourselves from the weather and predators, and build barriers to keep us safe. We have found ways to reduce the exposure to threats by analysing our environments, then influencing and controlling them to reduce the risk of harm to the things we value – sometimes going to extremes to protect them.

This is the simple distinction between humans and other animals:

- Animals *flee, fight or freeze* when confronted by harm and threats (the Three Fs).

- Humans will do the same, except we go to *extremes* in how we *calculate risk* and *control* the environment to remove the potential for harm and threats.

Risk assessment

How do we calculate risk in the modern world? You may have heard of a risk assessment, or even conducted one yourself. The ISO 31000 defines risk assessment as 'the overall process of risk identification, risk analysis, and risk evaluation'. The risk analysis component evaluates the potential and likelihood of a threat and looks at the consequences of the impact. The aim of a risk assessment is to make informed decisions about how the risk will be managed, to put steps in place to reduce or mitigate the risk, or, in some cases, to decide to ignore the risk.

The problem is that if you listed every type of potential threat, the list would be enormous. In the wider world, there's flood, fire, hurricane, terrorist attack, riots and cyber threats. In the workplace, there's intimidation, bullying, sexual harassment, violence, phishing, viruses, theft and leaking of sensitive information. Threats can also be felt in the supply chain, such as from fire, flood, port closure or material shortage (eg your supplier's cotton fields burned and you don't have another supply option).

The COVID-19 pandemic provided many examples of supply-chain risk, as factories had to suddenly close or operate on restrictive measures, with limited employees. The potential of a pandemic may have been captured in the risk assessment of these companies, but whether the likelihood of a threat was deemed low, or the impact underestimated, there would have been no risk treatment. The consequence is the exposure of the company to harm once the pandemic was realised.

Risk is subjective

Risk is about potential threat to our assets, but it is also about the value that a person (or group of people) place on an asset, and what they determine to be an acceptable level of harm to that asset.

Think about the devastating 2019–2020 bushfires that ravaged Australia, engulfing thousands of homes. The statistics from the Royal Commission are sobering. Thirty-three people tragically lost their lives in the bushfires and the bushfire smoke was responsible for an estimated further 445 deaths, not to mention that nearly three billion animals were killed or displaced. Over 3,000 homes were destroyed, with a national financial impact of over AUD $10 billion.[5]

Many people were forced to make a decision – stay and fight the fire, or flee to safer ground? The choice each person made was determined by many factors, including the perceived degree of threat (how close was the bushfire?), vulnerability (was the house made of wood or stone?), and the value each person placed in their house (was it a multigenerational family home, or a seldom-used holiday shack?). Some people fled and lost their homes, while others fought and risked or lost their lives. Each person had to make their own risk assessment.

When it comes to people's appetite and tolerance for risk, we are all different. For example, you may have heard the term 'control freak', meaning someone who feels the need to be across every detail, even when it seems extreme. They like to control all the variables, which they subconsciously see as vulnerabilities, to mitigate against potential harm. At the other end of the spectrum are the people who push the boundaries of risk, threat and harm. An example is 'adrenaline junkies' – people who participate in extreme sports, like base jumping, free solo mountain climbing or ice climbing. They have an appetite for risky activities that others would find fearful. Adrenaline junkies want to be able to achieve in an area that others fear to tread, and live to tell the tale. But they still make a personal risk assessment and many upskill and condition themselves before they proceed.

Risk can be quantitative – built on facts, simulations and probabilities. The decisions we make to manage or bear that risk are subjective and will vary from person to person, business to business, policy to policy. But at the centre, the common factor in risk is people, and this is why risk starts and ends with people. I also want you to keep in mind that, equally, *opportunity* starts and ends with people.

The Three Rs

In the business world, rightly or wrongly, most decisions for senior executives and boards are based on the Three Rs:

- Reputation

- Revenue

- Risk

If an organisation's risk planning fails and the worst happens, stakeholders lose confidence and trust in the organisation and its brand, and the reputation is damaged. This impacts revenue, which presents new risks, creating a vicious cycle that can pull a whole corporation down.

Have you ever wondered why 'people' are missing from this list? Especially when business is all about people? Businesses are formed and operated by people. Customers are people, as are investors and stakeholders. So why is it that people don't sit clearly as the number one priority? After all, they are the ones responsible for building a strong reputation, which can lead to improved revenue. They are also the ones creating the revenue and bearing responsibility for risks. And we have already ascertained that risk starts and ends with people.

It is a simple observation, but one that I find most challenging when I'm trying to engage those executives who are motivated by the Three Rs. These leaders tend to distance themselves from the topic of people, or at least they push those responsibilities down the executive ladder. But people and leadership are everyone's responsibility, and this must start at the top.

The stakes are high if you and your organisation are not focusing appropriately on your people. If your employees are not engaged and aligned with your organisation's values and mission, you are taking a huge risk. And risk is one of the Three Rs.

Reputation

When it comes to reputational risk, many of my clients fear becoming a headline – the subject of a shocking revelation that hits the media and dissolves all confidence in the organisation. But reputational risks go beyond headlines. They could include additional scrutiny and compliance measures, fines (organisation or individual) and even the possibility of jail for key players. Costs can mount up associated with defending allegations, including time and resources, legal and court costs, insurance increases and the difficulty of recruiting good people due to reputational damage and the perception of unattractive organisational values and culture.

Revenue

Customer and investor confidence are important when it comes to revenue, which is why the Three Rs go hand in hand and influence one another greatly. If your reputation is good, there are flow-on benefits to revenue. If risks are low, that helps the bottom line. Unfortunately, the opposite is also true – if your reputation is damaged or poor, it can impact revenue. If the organisational risk is high, you will incur additional risk management costs, and any risk incident could also impact reputation, which flows on to revenue, which flows on to risk, in a vicious cycle that can be difficult to escape.

CASE STUDY: Financial Services Royal Commission

In December 2017, the Australian Government established a Royal Commission to investigate allegations of misconduct in the banking, superannuation and financial services industry. The final report presented findings and recommendations relating to the dishonest conduct of several institutions and individuals. The findings included revelations that financial institutions were involved in money laundering and financing terrorism. Australia's major banks suffered enormous reputational damage in the wake of the Royal Commission, which led to lost revenue, huge costs and increased levels of risk.[6]

First, the banks lost customers. The damage and lack of confidence prompted many companies to leave the big four banks and explore second-tier financial institutions. Second, the Royal Commission led to increased scrutiny into the banks' risk management systems by governing bodies like APRA (Australian Prudential Regulation Authority), as well as new compliance measures and accountability. All of this was extremely costly for the banks to implement, on top of the enormous costs they had incurred in preparing their case for the Royal Commission. Third, the increased costs will need to be offset, either as job cuts, or in cuts to systems and technology, which will increase pressure on employees and potentially open them up to digital or personal compromise risks.

Risk

The human desire to avoid or reduce harm to things we value, whether they be people, places or things, has seen the rise of the risk industry, which is growing at a healthy rate globally. In 2018, it reached a value of USD \$65.9 billion (AUD \$92 billion), extending a period of annual growth in excess of 7%.[7] By 2026, the risk management market (a subgroup of the risk industry) is expected to reach \$18.5 billion globally, at 14.6% compound annual growth rate.[8]

An industry this large creates a competitive marketplace. There are many players and service providers and a great deal of noise and promises. Sometimes marketing is used to blur the lines around what products and services can actually deliver. Sometimes the truth gets stretched, especially concerning technology solutions.

Vendors may promise the world, but unfortunately, there is no silver bullet when it comes to risk management, and the goalposts keep moving. Executives, anxious to protect their assets and customers, are all too often receptive to these false promises, especially in highly technical areas where they may not have a deep enough understanding of the vulnerabilities and threats. As we will see in Chapter 2, executives face a two-pronged dilemma, being under pressure to protect their organisations from risk, as well as their own reputations as decision-makers. For many, their careers are on the line. These two prongs of risk, to the organisation and the individual, leave executives highly vulnerable to inflated marketing promises.

Smoke and mirrors

While the pressure on executives mounts, the focus on systems and technology to manage risk continues to grow rapidly. Rather than adopting a people-centred approach, the marketplace is filled with competitors offering high-tech solutions that most people struggle to understand. Jargon and complexity around how solutions are presented create what I call 'smoke and mirrors' solutions. Here are some examples I've come across:

- **Tick boxes** – Vendors use a tick-box approach to indicate what they can provide for customers. But the tick boxes are not explained or justified. Also, some of those boxes might relate to a shallow service offering, when a deep service is actually required.

- **Outdated offerings** – Vendors pull a range of products from their product suite to tick the boxes, even though the offered products are becoming legacy solutions. The effect is to imply a huge breadth and depth of services, when in reality the solution has been superseded and may be limited in scope.

- **Products that don't scale** – Vendors offer free licences to trial a product that might seem shiny and attractive on the surface, and even provide some value on basic-use cases. But once installed globally, the weaknesses of the product at scale and depth are exposed, leaving the customer with egg on their face. I have seen examples where customers needed to pull the product globally and then clean up the mess.

- **Black boxes** – Not to be confused with aeroplane versions, these often incorporate Big Data Analytics and Data-Driven Modelling to assist in automating and prioritising system alerts to announce when something is wrong. But they don't tell you anything about the trigger, the reason for the alert. In many cases, the alerts are false positives – the product seems to be catching a lot of errors, which creates distracting noise. This can cause some analysts to become complacent, though on closer inspection, some may not be false positives at all.

- **Fear tactics** – A concerning trend I have observed is when vendors and so-called risk experts use fear tactics to sell their solutions. Simon Sinek described an example of this in his book *Start with Why*,[9] where he called out IBM for using the phrase 'Nobody gets fired for buying IBM' to manipulate rational decision-making. The implication is that executives will be risking their careers if they go with an IBM competitor, appealing to a purely emotional fear response.

There are many losers in these scenarios, including the CISOs and the security teams who truly believed they had done the right thing and made the right choices for the business. Suddenly, the product fails and they find that, despite the shiny solution they've implemented, they're still vulnerable. Perhaps it prevents 70% or 80% of threats, but there's still a gap, or there are limitations to the solution that were not shared by the vendor, leaving the organisation vulnerable. You have to feel for the person who fronts up to the board and the executives to inform them of the failure and ask for more time and money to fix the issue. They're left discredited, disappointed, and vulnerable to risk.

Summary

Human beings have come a long way from the instinct towards flight, fight or freeze in response to a threat. Instead of reacting to immediate threats, we have the ability to proactively plan for risk and manipulate our environment to protect our assets.

In fact, we've been so successful at this that we've spawned a multi-billion-dollar risk management industry. Unfortunately, this same industry can sometimes seem to be more interested in hoodwinking us than helping us. At times, the industry exploits our real fears of failing our customers, our employees, losing our assets, or ending up on the front page of the newspaper in a scandal.

But the truth is that risk starts and ends with people. Only people could have made an art form of risk, and risk does not exist without people. No other species on our planet goes to such extreme measures to influence or control the environment to avoid risk. People calculate risk and assess its consequences. People use tools to offset risk, developing software, systems and defences to protect their precious assets. And yes, it is people, malicious or even ignorant individuals, that create risks to others.

By the end of this book, you'll understand how people are also the key to turning risk into reward. But first, let's take a look at what happens when risk spirals out of control.

2
The Risk Vortex

As humans, we have surpassed other animal species due to our combination of higher cognitive
capacity and advanced communication. This has also
elevated our ability to understand and control vulnerabilities and threats through risk management,
and has impacted how we view risk. In many ways,
our perception and management of risk has been
our secret weapon and has enabled us to survive in
the face of dangers that would have destroyed many
other species. Unfortunately, over the years, and
especially in the last few decades, our drive to influence and control risk has sometimes caused us to lose
focus, become distracted and for some, even spiral out
of control.

Many organisations have become trapped in what I refer to as a Risk Vortex. They have lost sight of their true mission and have instead become obsessed with one thing: risk management.

In this chapter, we'll take a closer look at the Risk Vortex. We'll examine its debilitating effects on every part of the organisation – employees, customers, leaders and regulators. We'll look at some simple questions that can help you determine if you have fallen into the Risk Vortex and, finally, you'll learn how you can escape from this vicious cycle.

What is the Risk Vortex?

When an organisation falls into the Risk Vortex, it feels like everyone is consumed with risk. A clear sign is when the focus and energy of the business has moved away from core business, when you find people are constantly second-guessing themselves and going beyond just pausing to consider risk factors in their work to improve customer experience. The Risk Vortex can also impact creativity, hampering people's ability to dream up better processes or to trial new product ideas and service offerings. Innovation teams may have to work with internal or external departments who are focused on risk assessment and management and who scrutinise their work efforts.

If you are in the Risk Vortex, it feels like the business has become so fixated on risk that no one can make a decision without tripping over risk factors. Risk assessment forms and checklists emerge from every department, posters go up on walls, new password protections are implemented, locks go on cupboards, new security protocols are introduced, warning alerts pop up and everything you do seems to be slowed down by invisible nets of increased security.

Meanwhile, the pressure on decision-makers grows. New threats seem to emerge daily in every direction and there are grave consequences for getting it wrong – after all, there's a duty to protect internal customers and clients from risks like hackers, identity theft, infections, fire or flood. Then there are regulatory requirements, which carry the risk of huge fines, legal costs and reputational damage if you fail to comply. Add to that the need to consider employee well-being, shareholder confidence and the expectations of the general community in terms of corporate responsibility and environmental protection and, at times, this creates huge levels of stress, becoming harmful to the well-being of the people responsible for managing all this risk.

The intensity around risk becomes so great in these organisations that specialised teams are formed, who are responsible for aspects of managing risk, ranging from Governance, Compliance, Legal and Investigation, to the Security Operation Centre (SOC) or CyberSOC (CSOC). Risk-based teams, like SOC and CSOC, are one of the fastest growing business units, but they can be costly and represent a heavy price for doing business.

How does the Risk Vortex affect an organisation?

The Risk Vortex may start small, but as risk takes over more of the daily focus than core business, it eventually finds a way to negatively affect the entire organisation and all of its stakeholders. The Risk Vortex is fed by both internal and external factors – let's take a look at them.

Employees

As the burden of managing risk increases, so does the red tape. Employees find themselves navigating the need for additional measures in areas like record-keeping, permission and access issues, lost passwords, new on-screen alerts and pop-ups, extra rubber stamps, and more risk assessments and consultation rounds. With the introduction of new processes and policies, the general level of paperwork fatigue increases, alongside irritation and aggravation.

People are forced to spend more of their time being sensitive to managing risk, at the expense of their primary roles. They lose confidence that they're on top of all the functional requirements and even start to second-guess themselves, as they don't want to make a mistake. They shy away from taking any initiative or tackling anything in a new way, as it's just too hard to navigate all the requirements. They can feel disillusioned or untrusted, and are often bored and less productive. Cracks can appear in their behaviour – they may become frustrated, aggressive, vindictive, ill or completely disengaged.

In terms of risk, when employees become disgruntled, it creates a highly volatile situation, which represents a potentially much greater threat than the organisation had been attempting to mitigate in the first place. At that moment, your own people can transform from your greatest asset to your greatest threat. We'll look at that more closely in the next chapter.

Customers

Customers expect and deserve a good – if not great – customer experience. They also need to be sure their best interests are being addressed, which is where security and risk management play a strong part. But when employees bear the burden of mitigating risk and navigating new processes to perform their daily tasks, it is the customers who feel the real impact. When employees are crippled by risk management, having additional expectations and processes to comply with, this results in a more involved process and response for customers.

Customers need to be heard and valued. If employees are struggling to keep up with the complex risk management expectations of the organisation, there is less time and less motivation to focus on the customer experience. If a customer wants something that is unusual or requires additional effort, it's easier to say 'no' than to enter the labyrinth of requirements to complete the request.

Leadership

Executives are under enormous pressure to make the right decision when it comes to risk. They must avoid reputational damage and protect their organisation from threats. They may employ people to help them explore the options and risks, and many rely on recommendations without fully understanding their implications. In recent years, there has been an increase in the number of industries becoming dependent on systems and technology. Technological developments are moving so quickly that it's difficult for executives to keep abreast of new capabilities and make informed decisions about the best options for the organisation. Yet they are still accountable for the decisions made, and may feel bombarded by expectations associated with protecting the organisation, customers and employees. They must avoid becoming a victim, being exploited, and ending up a damaging headline.

For many executives, risk has two prongs. On the one hand, there's the risk associated with normal operational business, things like protecting custom-ers and customer assets, protecting the business and business systems, protecting employees and creating a safe workplace. On the other hand, executives are also facing a personal risk – because their own careers are at stake if they fail to manage risk successfully.

All this pressure takes its toll. I've found that a lot of executives don't feel safe and supported in their roles. In many organisations, competition is aggres-sive and executives can feel as though rivals are out to get them, such as by leveraging the executives' mis-takes or failings, or sabotaging the executives' efforts to position themselves as a successor.

Fear can become associated with risk planning because the process of risk planning itself becomes a threat if it is not conducted and executed well. There may be a fear of failure, which poses a risk to the organisa-tion through second-guessed decisions, uninformed choices, or the avoidance of risk planning altogether. Some organisations also have cultural challenges that need to be overcome so that executives – and all employees – can feel safe to make the best plans and decisions for the organisation.

Regulators

The Risk Vortex is exacerbated when an organisation is in a heavily regulated industry, and/or is under great scrutiny. The intention of the regulators is to ensure the best interests of customers and stakeholders by overseeing and holding organisations accountable to market expectations and legal obligations. The Financial Services Royal Commission and the Aged Care Royal Commission are examples of where there were clear breaches in both market and legal obligations and the findings had significant impact on the Three Rs.[10] But changing legislative requirements, which carries the risk of heavy penalties for noncompliance, can create fear and hesitation.

CASE STUDY: Financial sector

Let's explore the Australian Royal Commission into Misconduct in the Banking, Superannuation and Financial Services Industry further.

If you reflect back to the earliest days of banking, they had what appeared to be quite a simple but important function. Fifty years ago, it was money in, money out. I remember going into a bank branch as a kid with my little bank book and the teller would write in the amount I was depositing, initial it and stamp it. That was the proof that the money had gone in. If I then took my bank book to another bank, the teller would say, 'Oh yes, we can see there's money in there.' I could withdraw the money, they'd initial it, stamp it, and that was proof that the money had gone out. It seems quaint and inefficient these days, but, nevertheless, that's how things were done.

With the advent of digital technology, all this hand-processing began to seem slow and cumbersome. It would take two weeks for a cheque to clear, and three business days to clear a deposit. That's because each transaction had to be checked by a person, on a working day. But as customers we wanted easier and quicker access to our money.

Customer expectations placed banks under pressure to respond to our demands, and to keep up with other services offered in the finance sector. The competition was fierce: if another bank could offer faster clearance of money, people were willing to change banks. We went from having hand-stamped bank books to computer terminals that connected to a central database. Your bank book would be printed with the amount of money you had in your bank account and you would be issued with a computerised statement.

As we know, communications and technology continued to evolve and customers have pushed banks to provide faster and better services. ATMs, EFTPOS transactions, online banking, mobile banking, contactless payments and mobile-linked accounts have all been introduced. Each of these innovations has increased speed and convenience, but every one of them has opened up chasms of vulnerability and risk.

Banks today offer a huge range of financial services, with accompanying risks around lending and investing in a volatile economy. The banks are hugely profitable, but they also have their necks on the line. They are responsible for protecting our money and play an important role in the stability of our economic system. This makes the banks accountable to the wider community as well. They can't be seen to be doing anything socially irresponsible. Their security and privacy systems are scrutinised, as well as their lending policies. Customers and the wider community have started asking questions about where their money is invested, in relation to matters such as environmental standards and labour policies. These changes have hit an industry that has to date been focused on one thing – making money.

When the culture inside banks exploded into the headlines in the wake of the Royal Commission, huge damage was done to the financial sector as a whole. The leaks concerning system vulnerabilities and threats seemed to be widespread. The reputational harm was enormous. Fraudulent employee activities were exposed. Customers were shocked and regulatory constraints were increased. There was a great loss of trust in banks, especially the larger banks, which just didn't seem to be in step with community standards and expectations.

The Royal Commission exacerbated the challenges of understanding and managing risk in the financial sector. This increased the size and velocity of the Risk Vortex for some banks, which are now struggling to take a step forward without assessing all business activities through a risk focus. The additional rigour and accountability changed the dynamics of the financial sector even more. Important questions need to be addressed when considering new business operations, not to mention improved skillsets for various risk-based teams, like security (SOC). This may require an increase in expertise, with researchers and knowledge specialists coming on board to advise in a multitude of areas.

Go back fifty years ago, and I wonder if the banks would have ever dreamt that their internal expertise would have moved so far past the basic requirement of money in, money out.

Are you in the Risk Vortex?

Take a moment to ponder the next few questions:

- Are you easily handling the assessment and management of risk, or is it continually dragging down your *productivity levels*?

- Is your organisation reducing risk effectively and efficiently, or are your employees' core competencies and *business functions impeded* by keeping risks at bay?

- Are you confident that your risk management approach is supporting your organisation's ability to *succeed in the marketplace*?

- Do you feel your organisation has become *distracted or overwhelmed* by managing risk?

- Is your organisation's risk management *cumbersome and costly*?

- Do you ever fear that the mismanagement of risk has the potential to damage your organisation's *reputation*?

How to escape the Risk Vortex

As we have seen, the vicious cycle of the Risk Vortex can have devastating consequences for many stakeholders. So what's the alternative? We must understand that risk starts and ends with people. People are not only at the centre of risk, but also the centre of any business – as employees, customers and shareholders. This means that people are also central to your escape from the Risk Vortex.

Creating an environment that allows your employees to feel safe and connected to the organisation and its success means they can become your greatest asset in risk management. If you get this right, your employees will actively 'protect the house' – your organisation. If you create an environment that is person-centred and eliminates the fear of failure, you will benefit from more engaged workers who put in the effort to succeed. They will be invested in the organisation's success, and will naturally work to identify threats and vulnerabilities, both internal and external.

It is your job to create a safe and supportive working environment rather than a harmful one. A safer working environment can reduce the organisation's risk profile and help you escape the Risk Vortex.

Summary

The Risk Vortex takes hold when an organisation becomes distracted by mitigating risk and loses focus on its core operations, when controlling the environment becomes more important than creativity, innovation and problem-solving. It can create a toxic environment where people are constantly dealing with red tape, scrutiny and other restrictions. The vicious cycle can be compounded by the expectations of regulators, investors, employees and customers – it begins to feel like every decision is about assessing risk. Everyone, from the customer service team to the CEO, can find themselves second-guessing decisions, feeling unsupported and vulnerable to exposure.

The way out of the Risk Vortex is through the power of your people. People can create the greatest risk (inadvertently or maliciously) as well as your greatest opportunity. They are essential to navigating your organisation out of the Risk Vortex. Keep reading to find out how, step by step.

PART TWO

PEOPLE ARE AT THE CENTRE OF RISK

3
System For Risk (S4R)

We've seen what happens when an organisation finds itself fixated on risk – it ends up in the Risk Vortex. But how do you escape from it? The first step is to understand how risk grows and develops, so you avoid falling victim to it.

In this chapter, we will unpack the powerful system we use to clarify how risk operates inside your organisation – S4R. It allows you to turn the risk dial all the way from being reactive, through proactive and predictive, to preventative. The system centres on people and the environments in which people interact, including the pressures and influences they are under.

Before we go into S4R, I want you to take a quick moment to think of a situation that you observed at home or work where an incident or accident occurred. When you read through this chapter, draw from that situation. We are going to go through an actual exercise in Chapter 5, but applying the principles here will already help you start looking at the situation from a different perspective.

Introducing the S4R

S4R involves three layers of understanding that extend out from the centre:

1. **People** are at the centre of our risk system (the inner circle).

2. **The Risk Lens** forms the second layer with two focal points:

   - Risk *to* a person

   - Risk *by* a person

3. **The Risk Model** is the third layer and takes a holistic approach to understanding what makes each person tick – what you could call their 'risk cocktail'. There are four key components to the model:

   - Predisposition – a person's life journey that influences how they interpret situations

   - Stressors – environmental factors that can affect a person, including home, work, finances and health

- Triggers – things and events that uniquely impact a person and can create stress

- Onset – the expression of a person's change in behaviour and attitude

The System for Risk – S4R

People are at the centre

Ensuring your people feel engaged and connected to the organisation is critical to people-centred risk management. Connection with your people exists on a spectrum from disgruntled and disengaged through to actively engaged. Disengagement can cause risks such as higher absenteeism or lack of productivity, or even theft and malicious attack. Moving to the other end of the spectrum – being actively engaged, empowering and motivating your people – can have many benefits. Engaged people protect your organisation and identify risks to help keep it safe. That is why people should be at the centre of your focus. They are critical when taking a balanced view to understanding and addressing risk.

People at the centre

The Risk Lens

The Risk Lens sharpens your focus as there are only two ways to view risk – risk *to* a person and risk *by* a person.

The Risk Lens

Risk *to* a person

Risk *to* a person occurs when a person is exposed to harm. This can come under two categories:

- **Natural** (aka Mother Nature) – examples include climate (weather, storms), terrain (mountains, deserts, rivers, ocean), natural disasters (tsunamis, droughts, fires, earthquakes) and wildlife (animals, insects, snakes, sharks).

- **Human-created** – examples include verbal abuse, bullying, physical violence, terrorism, shootings, fraud, theft, cyber-attacks (using technology as a weapon), explosives.

Risk *to* a person can be direct or indirect. For example, someone might witness an attack or murder, and even though they are not directly attacked, they may have a strong or traumatised reaction. This type of risk can also be found in the workplace. A person may be subjected to harm, such as bullying, intimidation, harassment or even a toxic work environment.

Risk *by* a person

Risk *by* a person is exactly as it sounds – a person who is inflicting harm. This is what you are trying to avoid happening to your organisation, both from external harm (by a person or people) and also from within.

Risk *by* a person is not always malicious. It can be accidental or can result from neglect. In the work environment, this is considered a type of insider threat and can be a result of a change in a person's attitude and behaviour. Perhaps the person has become disengaged and they are not paying attention, are making errors or doing poor work. Or they have become disgruntled and they express this change in damaging ways that can pose a serious risk to the organisation. This can come in many forms, for example an attack (physical, emotional, cyber), absenteeism, malicious damage, sabotage or theft.

The Risk Model

The Risk Model takes a holistic approach to understanding a person, how they are influenced by their environment and their risk profile. The Risk Model has four principles: predisposition, stressors, triggers and onset. These principles – ingredients, if you like – can help chart the journey an employee might take from being one of your greatest assets to one of your greatest threats. Each person has different ingredients in their cocktail, and it's not always possible to tell what they are. People don't wear labels to tell you what is going on inside!

The outer layer of S4R is the Risk Model

Predisposition

Identifying a person's predisposition means taking a holistic view of a person – basically, what makes them tick. Growing up, we are exposed to many different environments and circumstances that influence the way we perceive the world and ultimately, who we become as adults. When you think of predisposition, think of a person's life journey and everything that has influenced them along the way to make them who they are. Consider that humans are like sponges – we constantly absorb aspects of our environments as we interact and observe everything that is happening around us, both directly and indirectly.

There are many theories that explain how early development is influenced by our environment. Urie Bronfenbrenner's ecological systems theory identifies various ways environmental systems interact and influence our development.[11] At its most basic level, this theory explains how family, peers, school, religious institutions, culture, ethnicity, economic status and socio-historical events can all interact and influence a child's development and view of the world.

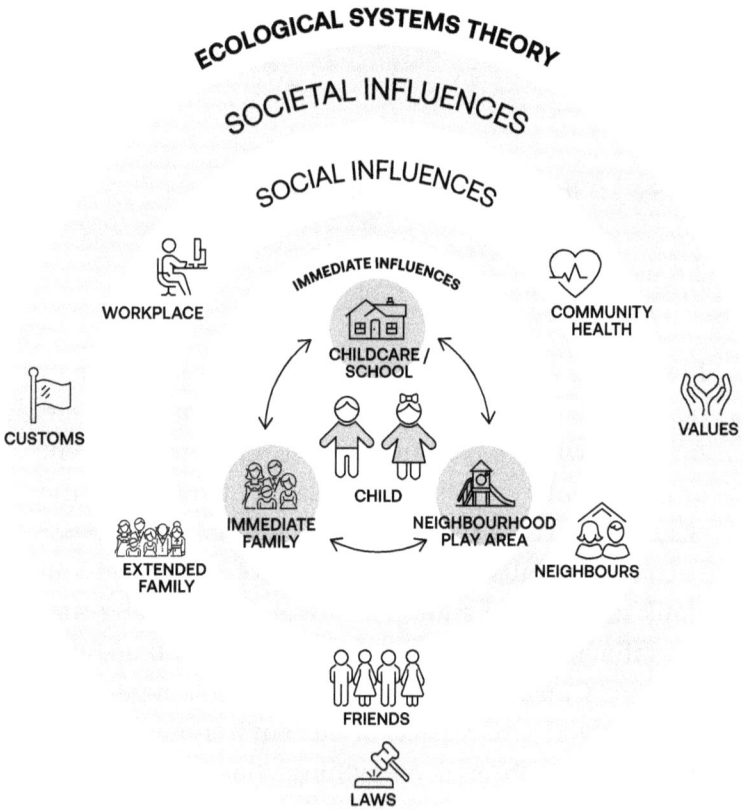

Ecological systems theory

The ecological systems theory describes how our experiences through life influence our development and contribute to our predispositions as adults.

Take a moment to think about your own life's journey, from when you were young, as far back as you can recall, to where you are today. I'm sure you can think of many influences from people, experiences and situations; or perhaps you can remember a challenge you experienced at some point, whether in health, work or your personal life. Your experiences will be mixed – some good, some bad and everything in between. There will be some moments that were life-defining, while others may not have been big moments, so long as they were important to you.

Have you ever reflected on your life like this and determined that you are now exactly where you are meant to be? Or perhaps you are surprised about where you have ended up in life? Have you ever challenged yourself on your own thinking and how you have been wired to think that way?

To understand a person's predisposition is not a quick personality assessment. It is much deeper and more comprehensive. People are truly fascinating and as much as we might see similarities in people, our individual life's journey makes us unique, which is why investing in understanding people better is critical and an important part of the Risk Model.

Contributors to predisposition

Our predispositions are affected by many factors:

- **Character** – Our internal selves and the values we hold close, including our morals, ethics and beliefs, which define the way we conduct ourselves.

- **Personality** – The part of ourselves or our qualities that the world sees, such as our extraversion, agreeableness, or conscientiousness. These traits can reflect our character, but not always.

- **Mental health** – Our emotional, psychological and social well-being, which impacts our ability to manage stress and maintain relationships with others. Everyone has challenges through life, which can affect our mental health, and cause mood changes, low energy levels, sleep problems, eating disorders or drug and alcohol use.

- **Emotional awareness** – Often grouped with mental health, this is our awareness of our feelings and our ability to manage them, such as through proactive changes, exercise or support networks.

- **Genetics** – Our genetic make-up can determine the likelihood of developing a particular disease or even exhibiting certain behaviours.

- **Physical** – Our ability to perform the basic and instrumental activities of daily living. This may be affected by disability, or levels of physical fitness. Some job roles have more demanding physical requirements, for example fire fighters, defence personnel or bricklayers.

- **Cognitive** – Our mental abilities, including learning, thinking, reasoning, remembering, problem-solving, decision-making and attention to detail.

- **Belief systems** – The principles by which we live and formulate our moral compass and ethics. These can dramatically influence our reactions and responses (either positively or negatively). They may be influenced by culture, an institution (eg religion), or the individual (personal and interpersonal).

- **Oppression** – Our experiences of injustice, harm or cruelty – whether actual or perceived – leading to a sense of mistreatment. We may, at some stage in our life journey, have experienced exploitation, marginalisation, powerlessness, cultural imperialism, violence or fear of violence.

- **Mindset** – Our frame of mind, which influences how we react to events and factors in our daily lives. Examples include having a positive outlook, being a pessimist, or being open to growth.

To give some insight into the influence of predispositions, in Chapter 4, I share a personal story of how the 2019–20 Australian bushfires affected me.

Baselines, buffers and buckets

People handle stress in different ways. We all have a level of stress in our lives as we navigate the various parts of it, such as home, work, personal relationships, health, kids, finances and community.

A person's predisposition, life experiences, skills and ability to manage stress all influence their baseline. The baseline is a person's status quo, how we would expect them to react and respond to normal daily activities and stressors. Everyone has a different baseline. There is usually a buffer in our baseline, which allows us to navigate minor daily ups and downs – we all have good and bad days.

Beyond Blue, a leading Australian mental health and well-being support organisation, uses the analogy of a 'stress bucket'.[12] The idea is to keep our stress bucket from overflowing. We all have a different capacity in our buckets, depending on our predispositions. Our ability to cope with additional stress depends on how well we are managing our life and stressors, and how far we already are from our baseline. 'Imagine you have a bucket. This bucket represents your capacity to cope with the ups and downs in your life. We all have a different sized bucket that's determined by a range of factors, like your genetics, personality and events that have happened to you.'

We all have our limit. The important thing is to recognise the signs that we are reaching it. Self-awareness can help us to protect ourselves both physically and emotionally from the harm that can result from stressors.

Stressors

Stressors are changing internal and external environmental factors that can create additional pressure, strain or tension.

- **Internal stressors** relate to a person's health, both mental and physical.

- **External stressors** include a person's work, family, home, social networks, community, society and financial situation.

Whether internal or external, stressors are environmental. And stressors are unavoidable. No matter which way you go – left, right, up or down – you encounter an environment with potential stressors. The moment you walk out the door in the morning, you navigate air quality, traffic, crowds and weather. Any of these things could add to your stress levels, which are different for each person. You might encounter a bee, and if you are allergic to bees, this will be more stressful for you than for someone who is not. When you arrive at work, someone could make a joke in the office. Everybody else might be laughing, but you may be furious because you find the joke rude or offensive.

Types of stressors

All levels of interaction with the world have the capacity to add to or reduce our stress. Environmental influences that may add to your stress burden include health concerns, relationship breakdown, workplace violence, legal or financial difficulties, or the loss of a loved one. These are just a few of the things that can impact a person's state of mind, and stressors like these cannot be left at the door when we come to work, despite the expectation of many organisations.

Triggers

A trigger is an event or interaction that impacts a person and can create stress. Triggers are as individual as a person's predisposition, which means they are not always obvious to others. Triggers can be an unpleasant event, including natural events like fires, floods or storms, or human-made events like robberies, relationship breakdowns or car accidents. Triggers in the workplace include redundancies, restructures, loss of team members or even being passed over for promotion.

There are times when an earlier incident in a person's life, which appears dormant, suddenly and powerfully awakens in response to some kind of trigger. It could be something as simple as an item on the news, or a passing conversation, that sets them off. The person, who has reached the limit of their stress capacity, snaps. Whether consciously or not, they do not think or behave in the same way that they did before.

CASE STUDY: Amy's trigger

Meet Amy, who has been struggling with red tape and internal bureaucracy. Beyond the frustrations of her own role, she has had to learn new systems and protocols because she has taken on a colleague's project while they're on leave. Due to problems at home (tensions in her marriage) and a recent knee injury that has kept her from her usual stress release of running, Amy is at the limit of her stress capacity. She is not thinking clearly and is feeling underappreciated, overworked and under pressure. When Amy's manager provides a performance review that is less than favourable, it is the last straw. She has an emotional outburst and resigns.

The trigger, the straw that broke the camel's back, was the poor performance review. But without the enormous stress levels that Amy was already carrying, she may have been able to cope with one unfavourable performance review. The emotional outburst and resignation represent the expression of her change in thinking, or onset, which we'll look at shortly.

Stress multipliers

Triggers don't always lead to an onset of behaviour change. For example, if a person is not close to the capacity of their stress bucket, the trigger and situation may become just another stressor in the stress bucket, without leading to an onset.

There are certain triggers that are far more likely to lead to an onset – often with velocity. These are stress multipliers. These types of triggers tend to strike a nerve in a person's belief system, such as their values and ethics, or are experienced as oppression. Examples include perceived attacks on religious or political beliefs, or sexual or racial harassment. Whether it is perceived or actual, these triggers have greater intensity than other stressors and will more likely lead to an onset.

It is also worth noting that if a situation or incident has touched on a belief system or oppression, it will usually be much more difficult to resolve. People find it difficult, if not impossible, to move forward from these issues. As a result, they may feel a heightened level of sensitivity around future communications, continue to harbour feelings of victimisation, and demonstrate exaggerated reactions and responses in their interactions.

Onset

When a trigger happens, a change occurs in a person's behaviour or attitude, whether consciously or unconsciously – it's a 'go or no-go' situation. If the response is 'go', the situation has moved to the point of onset. It is often when we see the move from risk *to* a person to risk *by* a person.

The onset is accompanied by an expression. Expressions are problematic and can lead to damaging outcomes. They can take various forms, including:

- Self-harm, such as drug or alcohol abuse

- Self-sabotage, such as losing motivation or spontaneously quitting your job

- Harm to another person, such as bullying or violence

- Harm to an organisation, such as stealing or damaging assets, sabotaging plans, disengagement or absenteeism

- Harm to the community, such as vandalism or gang violence

Regardless of the target, the expression of an onset tends to fall under two categories:

- **Observable** – the change in expression can be viewed in such forms as threats, property damage, violence, disgruntled or enraged outbursts

- **Concealed** – there is no noticeable change in expression, and perhaps a level of secrecy in the approach to conduct harm, which takes such forms as theft, embezzlement or capturing sensitive information or IP to take to a competitor

We'll look at how these different kinds of onsets can play out in Chapter 5.

Risk factors

There are a few additional considerations that should be explored when evaluating risk. These are:

- Time

- Environment

- Means, motive and opportunity

Time

Some people feel that if they leave difficult situations alone, the difficulty will dissipate over time and the people involved will 'get over it'. But sometimes the reverse happens – problems can fester when left unchecked. There appears to be two contradicting narratives:

- 'Time heals all wounds'
- 'Time exacerbates problems'

Each of these statements is true some of the time. Which one should you use?

If your strategy is to take no action at all, hoping that time will heal your problems, there's a good chance you are putting your organisation at risk. Once triggered, people may conceal behaviours that are extremely harmful to the organisation. That said, there are some cases where people's stressors *do* defuse over time.

My advice is this: don't make assumptions. Take the time to check in with your people in a supportive manner. It's the only way to discover whether an issue is festering or healing.

Environment

Environment refers to everything that surrounds a living being. To keep things simple, let's break it down into two categories:

- Natural environment
- Human-made environment

The natural environment relates to land, mountains, deserts, volcanoes, water, oceans, weather, climate, natural disasters, and so on.

The human-made environment includes tangible elements – cities, homes, manufacturing, transport, communication, appliances, technologies, conveniences and luxuries – and also the social environment, which is extremely influential in a person's life. Our social groups, communities, cultures, customs, organisations, laws and other social systems are essential to humanity flourishing, and heavily impact every individual person.

The workplace is no different. There are the operational requirements, which for a number of organisations is simply 'command and control'. There are also the social and cultural aspects, which include the values, behaviours and shared vision of the organisation. These can be strengths if employees connect to them, but in far too many cases, they are stressors.

Means, motive and opportunity

If you have ever watched a crime show, you'll probably have heard that to convict a criminal, the prosecuting lawyer requires evidence to prove 'means, motive and opportunity'.

- Means is the capacity to commit an act – for example, having the required skills, knowledge, tools, weapon and/or physical ability.

- Motive is the reason to commit the crime, or in our case, the expression – for example, a colleague sabotaging a deal to get revenge.

- Opportunity means the right circumstances – for example, the time and place, or ability to get access to commit the crime.

A lot can be learned from understanding means, motive and opportunity. When an incident takes place, many organisations are more concerned with removing the threat (employee) than learning about the person who caused the attack and their reasons for causing harm to the organisation.[13] But it's well worth taking the time to understand the underlying causes of a risk, as this is where risk countermeasures can be identified.

Implementing proactive measures in each area is important. For example, it is possible to reduce means and opportunity through things like digital restrictions or limiting access to a building or tools. As for addressing motive, a people-centred approach, forming connections with your people and lessening their potential stressors, can bring down their motivation to do harm.

Summary

Staying focused on the people at the centre of your risk management approach and strategy can make a world of difference. You can view them through the Risk Lens, which allows you to determine whether the risk is predominantly *to* a person or *by* a person, and where the two are connected. Most of the time, you will find there is risk *to* a person before there is risk *by* a person.

The Risk Lens underscores the importance of understanding the factors that feed into a person's risk cocktail. Every person has a unique level of ability to navigate particular environments. It is important to understand what risks may come with this, which is why the Risk Model contains four key components:

- **Predisposition** – A person's individual life experience, values, beliefs, personality, character, mindset, capacity for stress, and more, which affect how they interpret information and situations. Other factors such as genetics, environment and health can play a part in this as well. You can simplify this with the question, 'What makes this person tick?'

- **Stressors** – The internal and external environmental factors that create pressure, strain, or tension in a person's life. Internal stressors can be related to physical or mental health, and external stressors come from the environment around us.

These can include work, home life, social obligations or financial pressures.

- **Triggers** – The significant events that impact a person, directly or indirectly. There are human-made triggers, such as confrontations, bullying, violence and arguments, and natural triggers, such as fires, storms, floods and other natural disasters.

- **Onset** – The change in a person's attitude and/or behaviour after a trigger. This can be conscious or unconscious and can be a precursor to high-risk activities. Expressions of onsets vary in severity but can include harm to self or to others, a community or organisation. In any case, onset expression usually falls under two categories:

  - Concealed – when external changes in behaviour are not observed

  - Observable – when there are noticeable external changes in behaviour

In the next chapter, I'll introduce an analogy that makes the Risk Model almost frighteningly clear.

4
Russian Roulette

In the last chapter, we examined the Risk Model and took a holistic approach to understanding a person's risk profile. We outlined how a person's predisposition combined with stressors and a trigger can result in an onset and potential to express damaging behaviour.

To reinforce this model, there is a simple analogy that makes everything crystal clear – a game of Russian Roulette. In this chapter, we'll unpack the Russian Roulette analogy and look at some examples of how it plays out in the real world.

A deadly game of chance

Russian Roulette is a deadly game of chance involving a revolver, a bullet and some reckless players. A player loads at least one bullet into a revolver and spins the cylinder. They point the gun at the target and pull the trigger. If there's one bullet loaded, the gun has a one-in-six chance of discharging.

This powerful metaphor can be related to the Risk Model we covered in Chapter 3:

- **Predisposition** = the revolver

- **Stressors** = the bullets

- **Trigger** = the trigger

- **Onset** = the discharge

The revolver – predisposition

Like an unloaded gun, people are generally harmless when life is good and they're in a positive environment. They have the ability to do harm, but they have no reason or motive to do so.

This dormant capacity to do harm, represented by the unloaded gun, relates to what makes us tick – our values, beliefs, personality and all the other factors that contribute to how we interpret the world. In other words, our predisposition.

The bullets – stressors

So, how does our unloaded gun become loaded? Stressors provide ammunition for our revolver. Every time we are diagnosed with a health issue, or we encounter financial stress, relationship trouble, or tensions at work, it adds stress and the potential for a bullet to be added to the chamber of our metaphorical revolver.

You may recall, stress capacity is part of our predisposition, because we all manage it differently. Most of the time, depending on our individual character, we are able to carry on with our ordinary lives with a couple of bullets loaded. Many of us also have strategies to remove bullets from the gun, or reduce the likelihood of them being added, through activities like exercise, meditation or counselling.

The trigger – triggers

The trigger is, you guessed it, a trigger. As we saw in the last chapter, this can be an obvious event, or it can be something beyond your awareness, something you cannot see, appreciate or understand. Based on a person's predisposition and their life's journey, something as small as a news item or an off-colour joke could be the trigger, all the way through to a death in the family or a devastating bushfire.

In Russian Roulette, not every chamber is loaded with a bullet. If there is only one bullet in the gun, you have a pretty good chance that it will not discharge when triggered. But if there are multiple bullets in the chamber, your chances of a bullet firing from the gun when you pull the trigger increase. If the gun is fully loaded, you have no chance at all of escape.

Keep in mind that if the trigger is associated with a strong personal value or belief, or with feelings of oppression, the chance of aligning to a bullet are multiplied, even if there are only a couple of bullets in the revolver. That is because these sorts of triggers are stress multipliers and are more likely to set a person off on a path of destruction.

The discharge – onset

When the chamber is loaded and the trigger is pulled, the gun will go off, sending the projectile with velocity. This is the onset. The most important immediate concern is where the gun is aimed – its potential target, which could be:

- The individuals themselves through such acts as self-harm, depression, suicide, alcohol or substance abuse

- Other people – colleagues, friends, family members, authority figures

- Organisations – institutes, businesses, schools, government sectors

- Places or communities – parks, streets, social gatherings

At the point of discharge, damage or harm is already taking place. You can only triage the impact and consequences. If you want to mitigate or reduce the damage, the focus must be on stopping the gun from going off in the first place.

The best way to do this is to keep the bullets out of the gun. Being proactive to reduce the impact of harm in the employees' work environment by tackling both cause and effect is the best option. You must act early, when you or your team first become aware of changes that could take a stress toll on your people.

This is the meaning of people-centred risk management. But it does not mean you have to wrap a person in cotton wool. You need a balanced approach.

Examples of Russian Roulette

I've often used the Russian Roulette analogy and I've seen how useful it is in clarifying the ways that risk operates on people. It may initially appear confronting, but it provides a direct way of understanding how situations can quickly escalate into damaging events. Let's take a look at some real examples, starting with my own.

Example 1: Bushfires

During the terrible Australian bushfires of 2019–2020, I was personally devastated. For a start, I love animals, and, as part of my predisposition, I have a strong set of values around protecting vulnerable people and creatures. On their own, these traits were simply my unloaded revolver, my predisposition.

Before the bushfire season, I had been working in the public safety space in Canberra, advocating for proactive ways to reduce risks to communities and emergency responders – in other words, I had skin in the game. I had been frustrated by the bureaucracy that stood in the way of the safety of others, especially the emergency responders who were putting themselves in harm's way to protect our communities and national parks.

I knew, as did many others, that we were facing the threat of a bad fire season ahead. When the fires erupted, I was heartbroken by the devastation of so many communities I had been campaigning and working to protect, and I was terribly affected by the loss of wildlife – I couldn't bear to watch footage of koalas and other animals that had been burned. All of these factors added bullets – stressors – to my gun.

Combined with other stressors in my life, for example, my mother having a series of falls and needing to go into a high-care nursing home, I reached my stress capacity and there was damage to my emotional state. I became low, vulnerable and upset. I often found myself in tears as I watched the news and felt overwhelmed by a sense of helplessness.

It takes effort to look at yourself and develop the awareness. And I feel fortunate to have become self-aware of my emotional state. Being honest with yourself is hard and it's easy to dismiss our niggling concerns, to try and push through. Sometimes it is more difficult to recognise the symptoms because of the way we might be geared, as part of our predisposition.

My family saw that I was more emotional and became agitated. Initially, I struggled to find words to share what was happening with them. But my own self-exploration and drawing on the love of my family was grounding and helped my healing process. In fact, it was only once I put strategies in place, such as exercise, accessing my support networks, making personal donations, and letting people know I was available to help in any way, that I was able to find ways to start my own personal healing.

Example 2: Edward Snowden

Let's look at a different example, one that you may be familiar with – Edward Snowden, the infamous National Security Agency (NSA) contractor who many considered to be a whistle-blower, though he was definitely an example of an insider threat.[14]

Although Snowden's direct target was the NSA, the ensuing damage was felt by the broader intelligence and security community. His actions threatened the national security of the United States and put human lives at risk. The NSA and other intelligence communities suffered reputational and financial damages as well.

It is well documented that Snowden gradually became disillusioned in the NSA programs in which he was engaged. He observed matters that he felt were not ethical. Over a long time, he felt that his values and beliefs (part of his predisposition) were being compromised, adding more and more bullets to his gun. Snowden became frustrated and eventually he felt so strongly that he raised ethical concerns through internal channels (remember, threats to our beliefs and value system can create a stress multiplier). But his concerns appeared to fall on deaf ears and he felt ignored. The trigger was pulled.

From this moment, Snowden's behaviour changed and he went from expressing his concerns to concealing them, while he began to gather information, which he eventually leaked to the media. The gun had been discharged (onset), even though, of course, he was concealing his activities. There is an opportunity to learn from the Snowden case: concealed expressions can be extremely damaging and, in this case, devastating.

After the leak, when a thorough investigation took place, it became clear that the indicators (observable expressions) were there, but nobody had connected the dots, perhaps due to the culture within the NSA.

If Snowden's change in behaviour had been identified in time, his plans may have been discovered. Had he felt his concerns had been heard and addressed when he raised them, the trigger may not have been pulled, and it may have been possible to take some of the bullets out of his gun.

Common tools fall short

The Russian Roulette analogy is also useful for clarifying why some of the most popular tools in this space fall short. Let's take a look at some of them and find out why.

Assessing people

In an attempt to better understand their employees, many organisations have introduced testing as part of their recruitment process, including cognitive, aptitude or personality testing. Tools like the Myers–Briggs Type Indicator[15] or DISC[16] are used to help understand and improve self-awareness and communication with others both internally and externally.

But there are two main challenges to understanding more about the people we work with in this way. First, personality profiles offer only a limited view of a person's predisposition, which in our analogy is the unloaded gun. As we've discussed, an unloaded gun cannot cause harm – it is only when the gun is loaded with stressors, the bullets, that it can cause damage. The challenge with personality tests on their own is that they cannot determine the stressors that will operate on the employee in the workplace, nor do they take into consideration the individual's stress capacity. Personality is only one aspect of a person's predisposition.

The second problem is that these measures are limited and do not target core aspects of our identity or provide insight to our 'stress multipliers'. There are also privacy considerations meaning that organisations cannot ask certain questions. As we have seen, the most sensitive and volatile potential triggers and stressors are often related to our beliefs and oppressions.

Misleading recruitment

If a company's management is experiencing problems with workplace culture, they sometimes turn to Human Resources to explore their options. It can be common for organisations to use recruitment as a way to inject new blood to help rectify some of the existing issues. They want to bring particular capabilities and skills into the organisation to turn the culture around. They are looking for key talent to help them create the change they desire.

But the actual messaging used to draw in this talent may be an oversell of the current culture. It may express the organisation's desired image rather than its reality. People are often drawn to organisations with similar values to their own. By promoting these, an organisation may attract candidates under a fictitious promise. When the new recruits come on board and begin trying to work in the organisation's environment, they may find that they're up against an unexpected and potentially toxic culture, one that does not match the pitch they got and impedes their ability to be creative or innovative.

This type of scenario can lead to harmful stressors. The new recruits may think, 'Oh crap, they headhunted me – I had all these other employment options and I chose this company with its toxic culture and now I feel trapped.' Bullets could be loaded into the gun.

If your organisation is advertising a culture that is at odds with reality, you are running the risk of creating disengaged and disgruntled employees. This will ultimately lead to lower productivity and makes for a hostile work environment. Despite your best efforts to make cultural change, you may be creating the very environment you were trying to avoid. Unhealthy cultures and disengaged employees increase employee risk.

One-size-fits-all strategies

I have been privileged to work in various organisations as a people manager for a number of years, and I've found there are three categories people tend to fall into in the workplace. There are some who are really gung-ho, who are excited by a little bit of pressure and competition. There are a second group who don't want to be go-getters, who just want to enjoy their job, and do a good job, but they don't necessarily want to push themselves beyond doing their current job really well. Then there's a third group of people who are not meeting their job demands, whether that is related to their skillset, attitude, or just the result of a mismatch between them and their work environment and culture.

As a manager, it's your job to look after the people in *all three groups.*

You need to cater for those people who just want to put in a good day's work and collect their pay cheque, though there needs to be a balance, with perceived value on both sides (employee and organisation). The one thing you don't want is for people to feel as if they aren't valued because they are not willing to push themselves to excel. When people feel undervalued, they can become disengaged or even disgruntled, creating risk. A bullet can find its way into the chamber.

You also have to look after the competitive employees. These people want to overachieve and often like to deliver innovation and creativity. They will push to be the best and bring your organisation along with them. If these people are stifled or constrained, they become frustrated and even resentful or disgruntled. A bullet goes into the chamber. Though there is always the flip side of the coin, you need to make sure their enthusiasm does not mean they cut corners to get results or distract from business objectives.

Ideally, you'll have a mixture of both of these types of people in your organisation, which means you can't expect to keep everyone happy with a one-size-fits-all strategy. It is important to make yourself aware of people's predispositions, so you know what they value and what sorts of policies are going to do them harm. If you want a good starting goal to aim for, try this: do no harm to your people.

As for the third group, who are not meeting performance expectations, it is important to determine if the issue is the work environment, ie, is there risk to a person? The employees could have great potential, but may be working in the wrong environment or under a management style that does not align with them. If it is a skillset problem or the work environment does not suit them, then taking a fair and balanced approach, while looking after their well-being, can help the employees and the organisation find a way forward together. There are many ways this can be done, but the best ways normally require effort and patience.

Sometimes an individual may determine for themselves that they are not a good fit for the environment. If they feel safe and supported, you can work on a plan with them to help them find a more suitable role. Even if you have a disgruntled or hostile employee, a fair and balanced approach allows you to find a better outcome for the organisation. This person-centred approach enables you to take additional risk and security measures into consideration, to protect you from risk *by* a person. It also allows the organisation to keep its values and reputation intact.

Disarming the gun

Clearly, using the analogy of Russian Roulette, we don't want the gun to be discharged. Influencing aspects of a person's predisposition – the gun itself – can happen, but it takes time and can be difficult. If there's already a bullet lined up in the chamber, we can't stop it firing once the trigger is pulled. But we can work to prevent bullets from being loaded into the chamber in the first place. We do this by removing, or not adding, negative stressors.

In the workplace, we don't have control over every bullet. People will already have ammunition loaded from their home life, or from other areas of stress. But we can aim to ensure that the work environment does not add ammo to the barrel of the gun.

To do this, it's critical to learn more about the predispositions of the people on your team, to learn what is important to them. Even at the most basic level, you can gain valuable knowledge about how they like to work and what motivates them. You can then create an environment where you are at least doing no harm to the employee, ie not adding any bullets to their gun. You may even be able to positively promote their well-being.

Remember, though, that because of people's predispositions, there can be no one-size-fits-all solution. One example that I come across regularly is how people respond to work pressure. Some people react negatively to additional work pressure, while others find it energising and motivating. Either of these responses is natural and normal, and of course they occur on a sliding scale. Problems arise when we make assumptions about the way people are going to respond.

It's critical to remember this when we make decisions or communicate with our teams. Not everyone is going to interpret a message in the same way. If you assume employees feel negatively pressured by complex tasks, and remove the tasks, you may find some people become bored and unmotivated. But if you increase the number of complex tasks, some people may begin to feel stressed. Either way, you are increasing the risk of disengagement in one group of employees, and you could be adding bullets to the gun.

Transparent recruitment

Let's take another look at the recruitment process, because for many interested candidates and new starters, Human Resources is the first point of contact with the organisation besides digital engagement (website, articles). Setting the right message is important.

Earlier we covered how some workplaces pitch themselves as attractive environments to lure key talent when, in reality, the organisation has a toxic and problematic culture. Perhaps the culture being pitched is one the organisation aspires towards, rather than the one that currently exists. We saw that this strategy often backfires when new recruits discover that the workplace culture for the job they've accepted presents discouraging challenges. These new employees can become disgruntled and pose a threat to the organisation.

But how else can you attract talent to your organisation? A better way to approach this problem may be to bite the bullet (so to speak) and be up front about the cultural challenges. You can say, 'Hey, look. We are aiming to provide a safe and supportive workplace, but the truth is that we've got a bumpy road ahead before we get there. We actually need people who enjoy a challenge, and have the skills and personality required to turn around a toxic culture. We have some disgruntled people in the organisation, but we want to help them to step up and see what good can look like. We need people who can navigate the bumpy times and who can focus on that end goal with us, who can come up with innovative and inclusive ways to help us get there and bring others on the journey.'

Some people would run a mile if you told them this. They are the kinds of people who don't enjoy that type of challenge and stress. But some people would be excited by this challenge. I am one of those people. I'm a fix-it person. I like to walk into places that are broken. Throughout my career, people have sought me out to help them solve these issues. Even so, I can't tell you how many times the extent of the problem has been underemphasised. I frequently go into the organisation and find the situation is worse than described. A better approach is to be transparent, and to empower your new recruits to make changes and believe in themselves.

Revealing the truth about your organisational culture, warts and all, can make you vulnerable and is even scary. But if you are candid, and allow people to make a more informed decision, you have a much better chance of recruiting the people you need. You lower the risk of creating disgruntled employees, and you'll have a group of motivated people who are excited by, and committed to, the challenge of turning your workplace culture around with support from the organisation's leadership.

The key is to be transparent and authentic. It is not just about marketing and image. Let employees know that they are part of a team while still being clear on expectations. Don't just play up some fun-loving façade. The farce will eventually be exposed.

Summary

It takes just one revolver (the person), one round of ammunition in the chamber (the stressor), and one trigger to be pulled for a gun to be fired (the onset) and cause damage to your organisation.

As we've seen in this chapter, your own people have the potential to be weaponised against you if they are loaded with stressors. Hopefully you are thinking differently about the overall work environment at this point. You may now fully understand the expression that somebody is 'walking around like a loaded gun'.

Do you have loaded guns walking the hallways? If so, how many are there? How many triggers are being pulled? Have you been lucky with misfires, or have the projectiles already wreaked havoc on your workplace, causing damage? Is there an unending supply of ammunition, just waiting to be loaded and potentially discharged?

How can you help minimise this ammunition, and how can you remove active rounds from the chamber? How can you ensure that your environment is protecting people from harm, not causing people harm and turning them into loaded guns themselves?

The PROTECT framework provides a holistic method to answer these questions, which you will learn more about in Part Three. But first, let's take a closer look at person-centred risk by applying the principles of the Risk Model.

5
Starting With You

The best way to understand person-centred risk is to look at the ways stressful situations impact the people involved.

In this chapter, we'll apply the principles of the Risk Model to a situation in your own life, with a personal reflection exercise. We'll then broaden the perspective to look at how these situations affect other people around us, like friends and family, people in the workplace and even people we may have conflict with.

Are you ready? Then let's play.

SELF-REFLECTION EXERCISE

In this exercise, we'll apply both the Risk Model and the Russian Roulette analogy to a real situation in your life. You can use it to gain a deeper understanding of how predisposition (the gun), stressors (the bullets), the trigger and onset (the discharge) affect an individual – you.

Find a moment in a quiet place on your own to get comfortable. Take a few slow breaths and really centre yourself – once you've read the instructions below you might even like to set this book aside to focus and reflect. You may prefer to close your eyes for a bit.

Keep in mind this exercise is just for your private reflection and works best when you open yourself to being raw and honest.

Predisposition

Let's start by exploring your predisposition. What is important to you? What are the values and beliefs that drive you? How would you describe your character? Are you an optimist? Are you competitive? Are you a 'people person'?

Now picture yourself and the people in your life. What are your responsibilities and how are you managing them? Think about how you cope with stress. Use this as your baseline.

Stressors and triggers

Once you are there, think back to a moment when someone said or did something that caused a strong emotional reaction – perhaps you felt angry, upset or overwhelmed. We're looking for something that felt like a personal attack, where you went from 20km/h to 200km/h in a split second, an internal explosion. Maybe it affected you physically. Perhaps your body felt tense or heavier, or you suddenly felt nauseous. Perhaps your breathing changed slightly, or your heart began to race. You may have kept a completely calm exterior, but inside it hit a nerve.

Now consider, why did this have such an impact? Were you under a lot of pressure at the time due to other factors? Did the other person touch on a strong belief or value? Perhaps the person showed disrespect for your work ethic or moral principles. Maybe they dismissed you or your opinion completely. Perhaps the person was overly aggressive towards you. Do you recall what it was?

Onset

What happened next? Did you react? If so, was your reaction overt or concealed? Depending on the location, an outburst may not have been appropriate, for example, if you were at work. Maybe you didn't want the other person to know they had got under your skin. Or maybe you left the situation and planned your revenge.

Perhaps you expressed your feelings openly, maybe even in anger. Was it directed immediately at the person who triggered you, or did you walk away and find yourself acting agitated and aggressive with other people, such as colleagues or your family? Maybe you just recall feeling grumpy, withdrawn or disgruntled.

Think back to that time and your reaction. How long did the event influence you and your behaviour?

When you are ready and have completed the above reflection exercise, take some deep breaths and keep your situation in mind as you read on.

Self-reflection analysis

You've considered how your situation affected you in great detail. Now let's look at the same situation from the perspectives of others involved.

The other person

Why did they make their comments (which felt like an attack on you) in the first place? Are these sorts of interactions common in your relationship with this person? Or were they out of character? Did the person lash out and, if so, was it because they themselves were in pain or under pressure?

Is it possible that the other person was reacting to another incident entirely that had triggered them? Perhaps the attack on you was an onset and expression triggered by something else altogether – like something that happened at home or on the way to work.

If you had considered the possibility that the other person was expressing pent-up pain at the time, would your interpretation of the incident have changed? Would your trigger have been pulled? Or would this incident have made you think, instead, that something was seriously wrong in the other person's life?

Close friend or family member

Now let's think about a friend or family member who has been through, or is currently going through, a tough time. People react to life stresses in different ways. Perhaps this person has been unusually angry, depressed or unmotivated. Perhaps they have had a run-in with someone at work or at home and have been hanging on to a comment or action, and they're unable to let it go.

Maybe they aren't sleeping well, or have been drinking more than usual. Maybe they have been working hard, and when they're not working, they're exhausted and not pleasant to be around. Maybe they seem dismissive when people ask if they are OK? Maybe they have reached their stress capacity and are making erratic, ill-considered or out-of-character decisions. Maybe they're quick to anger, or quick to cry.

It does not take a rocket scientist to realise something is wrong. You might think, 'My friend isn't coping. When they have had issues like this in the past, they have been able to bounce back. This seems different.' You may feel ill-equipped to raise the subject, or support them, even though you can tell something is up. It's important to recognise that we all have skills in detecting the small changes in behaviour people exhibit when they are under pressure.

Colleague or employee

Many of us are quick to support a friend or family member when we sense, through these subtle signals, that they are going through a rough time. But how many of us apply these observational skills to the people around us at work?

Think of a time when you have given a close associate or direct report feedback that was not favourable, and it has not gone well. Perhaps you were baffled by the intensity of their reaction. Perhaps they seemed surprised, resentful or angry. They may have challenged you or vented frustration. Maybe the person walked away from the discussion and dismissed your comments. Maybe they went to lunch and didn't come back that day. Perhaps they decided that the problem was actually on your side and told themselves a story, that you were unaware of all the facts, or you did nothing to remove the red tape so they could fulfil their responsibilities.

What happens if you consider this incident through the lens of the Risk Model? For example, at any point, was their personal character, beliefs or values in the spotlight? Did your feedback touch on their performance, work quality, ethics, morals, integrity, effort, or ability to deliver results? By chance, had they been

working really hard, putting in the hours and trying to live up to the expectations of the business? Or
were they disengaged? Did they express any frustrations with organisational bureaucracy when trying to
deliver outcomes?

If you have said yes to any of these questions, and
you suddenly feel the need to justify your feedback
because it is all part of your job, then hit pause on that
thought just for a moment. This exercise is not about
your need to justify *your* approach, it is about recog-
nising potential triggers in others. You are no longer in
the centre, you are part of that person's work environment, and there may also be the possibility that you
are part of the person's social environment, especially
if they are also a friend.

After this feedback situation, was there an onset to
an observable expression or change in the person's
behaviour? Did they get upset, take the next day off
or suddenly ask for annual leave, fall sick, or, even
more dramatically, resign? Perhaps it was the opposite, that they seemed extremely calm and became less
engaged with you. Could there have been a concealed
expression?

The question to ask yourself is this: did my interaction with them pull a trigger in a game of Russian
Roulette?

Observable and concealed expressions

As we have seen, once the trigger is pulled on a loaded gun you can't stop it from firing. We also know that the expression of the onset of behaviour change may be observable or concealed.

Observable expressions seem obvious, but sometimes they feel like they have come out of nowhere because we haven't predicted them. Generally, an investigation into the onset of an observable expression captures comments like, 'No one saw it coming.' By the time the investigation is completed, indicators show that, in retrospect, it was clear that something was not right. Unfortunately, each indication (or expression) was likely viewed in isolation at the time, with no one connecting the dots until the observable expression occurred.

Concealed expressions present different challenges. The expression could come in the form of some kind of revenge, theft, fraud or even sabotage. You don't have to look too far to hear stories of a disgruntled employee who decided to take revenge on the organisation by causing harm in a public way, perhaps through the theft of customer details or by putting them on the dark web, resulting in a terrible headline and reputational damage.

Some employees are able to conceal their expression effectively. For example, a software engineer might take a stealth approach and create a 'backdoor' in software, which they exploit after leaving the organisation.

There are times when people try to conceal their expression but there is still an observable change in behaviour that appears out of character from their baseline. The person may not engage as much as normal (eg, they are not as talkative), or they may seem incredibly calm after an altercation with a colleague or manager that everyone is talking about. They might discreetly remove themselves from the team environment more regularly to conduct 'work' in private. Perhaps they frequently move out of the open plan workspace into an office or appear to go upstairs more often to collect print jobs from a remote printer, rather than using the local one.

These can be subtle changes in behaviour where the person is trying not to draw attention to themselves, even though they may be telling themselves a different story on the inside about how they feel victimised. Or worse, they are plotting revenge on a person or the organisation.

Does any of this sound familiar? I would be surprised if you said no, especially as a Gallup survey revealed that 85% of employees are not engaged in the workplace.[17] In fact, 81% of employees are considering leaving their job. So if you are telling yourself you aren't seeing the symptoms, then it might be time to pay more attention.

Disgruntled employees

Disgruntled employees pose one of the more serious risks to your organisation, so it doesn't hurt to keep an eye on the small signals that things are not going as well as they could be. Have you noticed anyone who appears disgruntled lately? If a person suddenly popped into your head, keep them in mind while we go over some questions to consider.

Think about when you first met them. Perhaps it was when they were initially employed – did they seem the same then? If they weren't always disgruntled, then think about how they behaved at the start. Were they normally a happy kind of person? Were they upbeat? Remember a person's predisposition also includes their attitude and mindset, which is often visible.

Have you seen a sudden change in their behaviour? Or perhaps a change slowly over time? Sometimes we may hear comments about a person like, 'That job is wearing them down.'

Could it be a stressor that has created this, perhaps the stress of the workload? Or perhaps it was after a run-in with the boss or a peer a few months back. On reflection, could that have been the trigger to the change in their attitude? Or has something significant impacted them in their personal life? Perhaps their personal relationship is strained and they are trying to work through the issues, but home feels like a war zone and work is intense, so they don't feel like they get a chance to really breathe. The outcome could be they don't feel valued at home or work.

Perhaps you see them struggling, or they seem agitated or even angry. They present as being disgruntled, unhappy, quiet or 'not their normal self'. Perhaps they don't feel they can do their job properly because of all the red tape – maybe they have complained about it. Regardless of the reason, if you have seen a change in behaviour, it is important to take notice.

Impact of employee disengagement

Employee disengagement can have major impact on your organisation's overall risk profile. Consider some of these issues that can arise from disengagement:

- **Higher absenteeism** – Regular or consistent absences can indicate that an individual is struggling with the current work environment. Their own productivity can plummet, and the workload then falls to others, who are forced to pick up the slack. This can generate even more stress for the person and other individuals. In some organisations, it can create a vicious cycle in which disengagement almost becomes contagious.

- **Lack of productivity** – Disengaged employees are at best satisfied with the bare minimum level of productivity. If engagement continues to decline, the entire organisation may suffer from their lacklustre performance.

- **Loss of organisational knowledge** – When employees disengage, they may leave the company entirely, taking with them their organisational knowledge. Then there is the investment to onboard a suitable replacement. There are huge costs – both monetary and performance-related – associated with searching, recruiting, and training new employees.

- **Loss of intellectual property (IP)** – Proprietary knowledge can be taken elsewhere, either through theft (insider threat) or if the employee signs with a competitor (external threat).

Summary

We're all familiar with the strong emotions that are triggered when someone makes a personal attack on our beliefs or values, but sometimes we forget that other people are also experiencing their own emotional reactions.

Usually, the clues are there in the way people are behaving, but the managers are not paying attention to them. Ignoring those signs of harm may mean you miss the escalation that occurs when further stressors hit (risk *to* a person). This could lead to the employee becoming disengaged, disgruntled, unfocused and neglectful of their responsibilities, or acting out maliciously and causing harm to the organisation (risk *by* a person).

But there is often huge opportunity to increase employee engagement. Employees are looking for connection with the organisation and most people want to have their voices heard. If employees see and believe their feedback is being listened to and taken seriously, and there is genuine interest in their well-being, they will feel like a part of the picture rather than just a cog in the machine.

In this chapter, we've seen how stressors play out in the lives of real people, and the importance of paying attention to the signals when people are acting out of character. Next, we'll look at the active steps you can take to reduce the stressors on the people in your workplace.

PART THREE
PROTECT THE HOUSE

6
The Safe Zone

Our commitment to all our clients is to help them find ways to 'protect the house', ie the whole business: its people, assets, brand and reputation. We approach this using our PROTECT framework, which provides a powerful method to turn the dial from being reactive to risk, to proactive, predictive and ultimately preventative.

By forming this connection with your people and tapping into their desire to protect the house, you will find they will proactively notify you of potential threats as soon as they identify them, working as 'risk sensors' for the organisation.

Are you ready to start turning your risk into opportunity? Here in Part 3, I'm going to share the thinking behind the evidence-informed PROTECT framework, which was developed using our people-centred risk system S4R to drive transformational outcomes for organisations by mitigating risk and opening up opportunities. First, I'll introduce you to the Safe Zone, the foundation for PROTECT, then in Chapters 8 and 9, we'll look at the PROTECT framework itself.

Let's start by looking at why it's imperative to create a Safe Zone in your organisation if you wish to actively take preventative measures to address risk. We'll explore how to do this, and take you through some examples of what a functioning Safe Zone looks like.

The Safe Zone

By the very nature of our work in risk management, my team and I often find ourselves working with our clients in the most sensitive aspects of their business. Our job is to seek out vulnerabilities and discover areas where our clients would suffer the most damage if they were threatened. There is no way that we could do this work if our clients did not have confidence and trust in us. This is why the first thing we do when we begin working with a new client is to establish a Safe Zone.

As part of the Safe Zone, the environment we look to create is focused only on the client. We have no agenda other than supporting them. For example, we do *not* use their name and brand in our case studies – we are there for their benefit alone. This is why when you read our case studies, we share the value of insights and knowledge. We don't share the details of the client.

This has become a foundational principle for our work. We focus only on our clients' needs and never boast about the clients we are working with. A doctor cannot treat a patient if the patient does not feel safe enough to disclose their symptoms. So we create a safe space around ourselves and our clients, almost like an incubator, where our client knows we are totally focused on them. This is the Safe Zone.

Organisations also need a Safe Zone

We educate and encourage organisations to create Safe Zones in their business. People working together need to be able to trust that they can expose their vulnerabilities and sensitivities without fear that they will be later used as weapons against them. Without a Safe Zone, people will hide and cover up vulnerabilities and areas of concern, rather than openly addressing them, and this can only have dire consequences for the organisation.

The Safe Zone is designed to get the best from all participants, without fear of failure. It creates the conditions for people to be able to make mistakes as they learn, grow and push their skills or performance limits. This does not mean that the Safe Zone encourages poor performance – in fact, the opposite is true. A Safe Zone is a proactive way to approach risk and people, knowing that people do make mistakes, especially under certain circumstances, such as when they take on a new role or skills. With a Safe Zone, you factor this into the work environment.

Unfortunately, many organisations do not create a Safe Zone for their teams. This means that for their employees, the workplace is filled with the potential risk of exposure. And as we have seen, risks *to* a person can quickly transition to risks *by* a person.

Risk in a Safe Zone

While a Safe Zone contributes to a more motivated, innovative and supportive work culture generally, it's important for organisations to create a Safe Zone particularly in relation to risk. Risk is such a sensitive area that people must feel safe to speak freely, so that they can alert you when they've noticed a vulnerability in the organisation or discovered a potential threat. They can bring it up, talk about it and work it through without needing to blame someone, save face or find a scapegoat.

In many situations, vulnerabilities and threats are known to employees, but no one acts on them.

Typically, an organisation suffers an incident or disaster and then investigates what went wrong after the fact, as a reactive measure. At this point, it is not uncommon for people to start throwing one another under the bus, deflecting the spotlight from themselves. The investigation might discover that many people knew the threat or vulnerability existed, but no one spoke up for fear of the consequences. Speaking up would have revealed that someone had failed, and in many organisations, failure is not acceptable.

CASE STUDY: JFK

Have you ever watched John F Kennedy's famous Moon Speech?[18] More than just a speech, JFK's message was a pitch, and a bold one at that. It is one that certainly would have lured me in. It resonates with my passion for pushing boundaries and my constant desire to make positive changes. Choosing to go to the moon demands collaboration and cooperation. It asks citizens not to focus on what could go wrong, but to set expectations above and beyond what was previously thought possible – even if the challenge is a great one.

Kennedy wasn't pitching to a corporation; he was pitching to a nation. But like the CEO of a company, he had a vision and a mission. His speech was a rallying cry to the country. This was leadership by inspiration and commitment to a task beyond the skills and knowledge of that time. He gave a clear and focused goal, and did not shy away from the fact that it was the 'most

---

hazardous and dangerous and greatest adventure on which man has ever embarked'. There were going to be many obstacles that those involved would need to overcome with the best of their energies and skills, not to mention an act of faith and vision, but he made it clear to the country 'we are all in this together'.

The JFK speech was successful in luring many types of skilled and motivated people to the moon program. But consider the type of work environment they were entering. They were the first to ever attempt such a feat, with the eyes of the nation – the eyes of the whole world – watching their every step.

Think about the pressure. Now think about the era in which this took place. Technology was far more primitive than what we have today, and these brave people were responsible for getting men to the moon. There were accidents along the way, and many people found themselves drained, anxious and unhealthy. The cost of landing on the moon took a toll on many people. But somehow, they succeeded. How?

The difference between JFK and many CEOs is that Kennedy was brutally honest about his expectations. He didn't use marketing spin and lingo to make the task seem easier than it was going to be. He knew from the start that this was going to be a challenge, that there would be mistakes made along the way, and he was as transparent as he could possibly be about that. Still, people rallied around him because his pitch was aimed directly at people who were energised, not daunted, by the scale of the challenge. They understood that they would have to stumble and fail at times, and they would need the faith to get back up and try again. They were doing it not because it was easy, but because it was hard, and they knew that their president was backing their efforts to succeed.

How to create a Safe Zone

So how do you create a Safe Zone? The secret is that you must allow people to feel safe to make mistakes and even dare to fail.

You must create an environment where people can feel free to fail, because it's only when there is space to make mistakes, miss the mark, learn lessons and move on that people are able to risk what it takes to succeed. Only when people are supported to get back on their feet after a fall will they, in turn, support the organisation to bounce back from its setbacks. This is not about being expected to accept poor behaviour, attitude or performance – it is about setting people up for success as they develop and expand their skills. There are ways to do this without heavy exposure to the organisation.

The idea of having people learn from mistakes or even failing when stretching themselves is not new. Adaptive approaches to innovation, allowing employees to push creative boundaries and aim for breakthroughs are encouraged in a number of industries, like software, though it's clear that if you don't invest in the right approach and mindset it can be hit and miss. It's critical, in whatever method you adopt, to explore failures as growth opportunities.

The adaptive framework Agile is a method of project management used especially for software development.[19] Agile is characterised by the division of tasks into short phases of work and frequent reassessment and adaptation of plans, often referred to as a pivot. Some organisations in other industries are also using Agile principles and project management techniques, due to the value of being able to make decisions earlier in the project and adapt plans if needed.

There is also the 'fail fast' philosophy,[20] or even 'fail fast, fail often'.[21] But a word of caution: if you are only leveraging the concept and language to promote the idea of a safe work environment in which 'dare to fail' is part without having implemented the structure to set people up for success, then it is likely to end badly. 'Failing well' is another concept that requires a shift in mindset to continuously learn and apply what you have learned.

Atlassian, a global software company focused on helping teams to collaborate, build and recreate, shared in one of their blogs that 'embracing failure' isn't a case of 'calling failure out, it's more like: of course, that's part of being in action.'[22] Changing both the mindset and the language is vital.

Many well-known brands have openly shared experiences and learnings from failure. According to an article titled 'How Coca-Cola, Netflix, and Amazon Learn from Failure' in the *Harvard Business Review*, 'too many leaders live in fear of mistakes, missteps, and disappointments. But if you're not prepared to fail, you're not prepared to learn.'[23]

The objective is to encourage employees to stretch themselves, to allow innovation to be part of the workplace mindset and recognise when something isn't working. But it is critical to grow from the experience. In a Safe Zone, this learning supports individuals and teams to succeed.

Keep in mind that being innovative does not have to always mean the development of a new product or service. We can also innovate in our approach and processes for servicing internal and external customers.

It's always going to be scary the first time you try to create a Safe Zone. It's like most things that are new – there will be a certain element of fear. To achieve it, you must have faith in the process, and you have to be comfortable being uncomfortable. You must be willing to be vulnerable, and to allow people to step up in ways that they have never done. You've got to ask them to be transparent where they haven't been before. And everyone's going to feel really nervous, because everyone will be vulnerable and may feel exposed. If there are vulnerability and threats, you can't hide them anymore.

When you create an environment that allows people to feel safe to stretch themselves and contribute in a respectful manner, you will see a focus towards the best interests of the organisation. In the right environment, people's successes are not based on sabotaging one another, or capitalising on one another's mistakes. People will not conceal their own mistakes, hoard resources or withhold information to gain advantage. Instead, you will create an environment where they are empowered to bring their best efforts, by free choice. It is only when people feel safe to fail, that they also feel safe to succeed.

Training wheels

We've seen that it's important to create a safe work environment and culture where stumbling and failure can be a pathway to success. We need to put in protective measures to support people in areas where there is a high risk of failure. These measures are your training wheels.

If you are asking your people to step up, to take on new responsibilities, or to extend into a new area, you've got to put those training wheels on. This is because we all know that when we do something new, we are going to make mistakes. And often people learn quicker through making those mistakes, so you need to support your people and protect your business from these entirely predictable blunders.

For example, you may provide additional training or a mentor, you might introduce a temporary QA check, extra briefing sessions, specialist advisors, extended deadlines, or an increased project budget to allow for contingencies.

When you introduce these additional measures to help your people, they will actually feel more supported, engaged and motivated to step up and give new things a go. You'll be communicating to your people that you understand that there is a possibility of errors or failure, but that you have their backs, and you believe that they have the capacity to succeed. In other words, you're creating the ideal conditions for success, without the fear of failure.

CASE STUDY: Three men walk into the jungle...

Some time back, I was privileged to work with a large global organisation's management team to resolve a complex issue relating to vexatious black box alerts in their security system. The solution my team developed for them used left-field thinking. It involved specialised analytics, which included leveraging the power of a probabilistic model known as a Bayesian Network.

As we tried to explain our approach, even to my ears, we started to sound academic and inaccessible. Our initial messaging sounded just like the sort of 'smoke and mirrors' that unscrupulous risk consultants use to bamboozle their clients into purchasing solutions that they don't understand.

That is not how I like to operate. I knew it was important to educate them through a common language. We brought in a scientist with a PhD in probability theories and Bayesian Networks, which seemed intimidating at first, but when the scientist opened his presentation on what most would consider a dry subject, it sounded like a joke: 'There were three men walking in a jungle...'

Smiles broke out. People started to pay a little bit more attention. Our scientist's approach did two things. First, it quickly gave the management and project team an insight into how the system would work – using an analogy of three people's points of view when encountering the same object from different starting points. And second, it changed the atmosphere in the room into a Safe Zone. It broke down the barriers and encouraged people to ask questions.

I believe that if I cannot clearly articulate a solution so that my client understands it thoroughly, then all I'm providing is smoke and mirrors. We were bringing in a sophisticated and somewhat complex way of solving their problem. We needed to create a space in which it was OK to ask questions, even so-called 'stupid' questions – not that there is such a thing. We wanted the client to understand the approach and solution we were proposing so they could make an informed choice and give us granular feedback on whether or not the solution would be right for them.

By the time we got through the first couple of meetings, everybody felt comfortable and free to speak, which was really important, because they began to share more. They told us about their frustration with previous solutions and the ways in which other systems had failed to solve their problem. This helped us to make massive inroads and analyse how they were approaching some of these risks, threats and vulnerabilities through a different lens. By opening ourselves to questioning and critique, we were rewarded with confidence, trust and a much deeper understanding of the vulnerabilities the organisation was facing.

I have a rule: we must practise what we preach. If we're asking organisations to let us in, and share an area where they're vulnerable, we too have to be vulnerable. It's critical that our clients know that it is OK to challenge us, but it's also vital in a Safe Zone that there is a common language and clarity, so no one gets left behind.

What does a functioning Safe Zone look like?

You may be wondering how it feels to work in a Safe Zone. Here are some of the hallmarks of an organisation that's got it right.

1. **It's safe to succeed without fear of failure.**

   As we've seen, the main sign that an organisation is operating in a Safe Zone is that people feel safe to stumble and even fail at times as they stretch themselves to contribute, grow and succeed at work. The saying 'we learn from our mistakes' is true – it is often when we learn the most. We just need to introduce the training wheels to protect both your people and the business. It is also important that everyone in the business feels that help is there for them and they don't have to delay asking for it.

2. **There is open and respectful communication – both ways.**

   In an organisation operating in a Safe Zone, people actually talk *to* one another instead of *at* one another. They have confidence in their ability to share comments in a respectful and meaningful way. People feel safe to openly communicate observations or concerns without fear of repercussions. This also helps with collaboration, gathering feedback and allowing people to share when they are observing an emerging or possible threat.

3. **People have organisational pride.**

   Employees working for an organisation operating in a Safe Zone tend to be motivated and energised by coming to work. They're there because they feel they have purpose and a sense of pride contributing to the success of the company and its well-being. They feel they are making a difference in an ethical, transparent and honourable way. They have the freedom to bring their best ideas, solutions and creative thinking to the organisation, without the fear of failure.

4. **Mistakes are treated as opportunities for continual improvement.**

People are allowed to make mistakes and learn lessons from them. In fact, Safe Zone organisations almost celebrate the lessons learned. They encourage people to share the story of what they learned (both as an individual and as part of a team) and how they have improved. People share what they believed to be successful and are able to celebrate how far they have come with the wider team.

The commitment to this type of transparency goes beyond lip service or just words of encouragement – it's cultural. Here, fear of failure is no longer a barrier to trying or succeeding.

5. **Employees gain more than just job satisfaction.**

This might sound soft and fluffy, but given that emotions drive motivation, if you look after the well-being of your employees, they will respond in kind. Identify and remove the areas where your organisation is doing harm to its people and reap the benefits. It is exciting when you see people transition to feeling safe to openly share their ideas, as they begin to identify, manage and even prevent harm being done to the organisation.

Summary

One of the fundamental steps in positively turning the dial on risk management is creating a Safe Zone. This can be a challenge in organisations that have a punitive or adversarial culture. But if people in your organisation experience negative consequences when they fail, there is no incentive for them to work collaboratively to reduce risk. Instead, you're encouraging a culture of concealment, secrecy, cover-ups, blame-shifting and scapegoating. Not only is this a toxic environment in which to work, it also means you create blind spots of internal risk, which become almost impossible to identify or mitigate.

The best way to create a Safe Zone is to build an environment that allows people to feel safe to succeed without fear of failure, and without ramifications on the business. Treat your people's growth and progress as a learning tool and encourage and support them, especially when they are stepping into new fields or responsibilities. In other words, give them training wheels. Because it's only when people feel safe to fail, that they also feel safe to succeed.

Once you have removed the fear associated with failure, you may find that the culture in your organisation begins to shift. If you invest in your people's growth and well-being and support them while they stretch themselves, then they tend to reciprocate and feel connected to the organisation and its success, often with a sense of pride.

7
PROTECT – Step One

So far, we've looked at the importance of placing people at the centre of risk. And we've seen how neglecting people, failing to connect with them, or requiring them to work in a toxic workplace culture can have a devastating impact on your organisation. But how exactly do you go about turning this around?

Once you've established a Safe Zone in which people feel safe to fail as well as to succeed, next, you can begin to implement the PROTECT framework, which I'll present to you over the next two chapters. Here in Step One, we'll look at how to leverage the first three aspects – people, the Risk Lens and the origin of risk – to protect your organisation from risk. In Step Two, we'll look at the final four elements – trust, environment, collaboration and toolkit.

Introducing the PROTECT framework

When you hear the words 'protect the house', what do you think of? Hopefully they make you think about protecting everything that is valuable and important to you. The 'house' is symbolic of an organisation, department, agency or home. The PROTECT framework is about uniting all stakeholders in the 'house' to focus on protecting what is important.

By implementing this framework, you can create a workplace where each person feels more connected and has the opportunity to actively contribute. They will be motivated and galvanised to defend the organisation from harm as though it was their own home.

PROTECT is the acronym for our comprehensive, balanced and evidence-informed approach to understanding and addressing risk, through the seven principles listed below:

- **P**eople
- **R**isk Lens
- **O**rigin (of risk)
- **T**rust
- **E**nvironment
- **C**ollaboration
- **T**oolkit

P|R|O|T|E|C|T
THE HOUSE

PREDISPOSITION

STRESSORS

RISK TO A PERSON

RISK BY A PERSON

ONSET

TRIGGERS

P
PEOPLE

Activate your people to become your greatest risk management asset, not your greatest risk.

R
RISK LENS

People are at the centre of risk and risk falls under two categories:
1. Risk to a person
2. Risk by a person

O
ORIGIN

The origin of risk is presented through the Unearth Risk Model which consists of four principles:
1. Predisposition
2. Stressors
3. Triggers
4. Onset

T
TRUST

Build confidence through your people.

E
ENVIRONMENT

Maximise the work environment.

C
COLLABORATION

A "win with" mindset empowers collaboration as one team and forms a common language for clarity.

T
TOOL KIT

Right tools for the right job. Expertise, skills, knowledge, processes and innovative technology capabilities.

The PROTECT Framework

As we saw in Chapter 3, the foundation of our framework is the system for risk, S4R, where people are at the centre, viewed through the Risk Lens. By looking at each person's 'risk cocktail' (risk model), we can understand the origin of risk. These three aspects – People, Risk Lens, Origin – make up the PRO section of the PROTECT framework. Let's explore how you can work with these three categories to protect your organisation.

People

Everything about risk comes back to people. If you don't put your people first, you are at risk of creating problems, ranging from a disengaged workforce to insider threats, bullying, workplace violence or intimidation. Disengagement is common and can take the form of lack of motivation, absenteeism, feeling overwhelmed, depression, bullying and generally not coping well. Mental Health Australia's 2018 report found that the cost of workplace mental ill-health to Australia in 2015–16 was $12.8 billion, including $2.6 billion in absenteeism and $9.9 billion in presenteeism (reduced productivity).[24]

Checking in with employees is important. By starting a conversation and commenting on the changes you've noticed, you could help an employee or workmate open up, though having the skills to support them if something is wrong can seem daunting.

Many organisations have support through Human Resources or third-party groups, but if you do not, then organisations like 'R U OK' can provide steps to help.[25]

Let's look at why employees become disengaged. Sometimes they are affected by personal issues outside of work, but often it is challenges in the work environment that are causing them to disengage. Many organisations take a reactive approach when employees do this. That is, they only deal with the issue after an incident has occurred. But the cost of failing to address the issues and the pain of managing the fallout far outweighs the investment of time, money and effort it would take to get it right earlier in the process.

Turning the dial towards PROactive

Going back to the Risk Model, when an employee shares a sense of frustration, it is not a foregone conclusion that this will reach the point of a trigger being pulled, but it can certainly be adding to their stress bucket. An expression of frustration is an important opportunity for a manager to follow the thread of an issue to examine the touchpoints where the pain is being felt for the employee. These are the places where an employee interacts with operational processes, policies and governance responsibilities, customers (internal and external), or with technology.

CASE STUDY: Touchpoints

Henry manages a sales team at a branding agency that engages clients. The sales team secures an opportunity, then transitions the client to a project management team to oversee the execution of the project. One member of Henry's team, Sanjay, is normally a bright and happy person, but lately he has become withdrawn. A couple of weeks ago, Sanjay made a comment about the lack of communication between the project management team and some of his recent clients that he had passed on to them. Henry explained it was all a standard process and the project management team were well equipped to service the client, and there was nothing out of the ordinary with the type of project. Sanjay appeared to accept this and made no further mention of it.

Soon after the conversation, Sanjay called in sick a few times. He hasn't been contributing in meetings and his performance has fallen. Concerned, Henry invites him out of the office for a coffee. He says 'Hey, I've noticed you seem a little low lately. Is there anything you want to share with me, either something at work, or at home? We want to make sure that we can support you.'

Sanjay is touched that Henry has reached out. He confides that he feels overwhelmed and unmotivated. Henry suggests that he could spend a day with Sanjay to take a look at what's going on. Henry makes it clear that his suggestion is not about performance management, it's about looking after Sanjay's well-being and improving Henry's understanding of the business.

Sanjay agrees and Henry spends a day with Sanjay. He discovers that many of the calls Sanjay receives from clients are about frustrations with the project management team. This touchpoint is turning into a major source of stress for Sanjay, not to mention indicating a potential symptom of concern in another part of the business. The clients are complaining about delays in their projects and the lack of communication from the project team. The clients are turning to their only other contact in the organisation – Sanjay – to find out why their projects have stalled. Some of them express their anger and frustration and imply that Sanjay is incompetent.

Henry had no idea this problem existed. He decides to meet with the project team's manager, who follows up with all the disgruntled customers immediately and provides additional support to the project teams that might be struggling. He also agrees to get the sales and project-management teams together regularly for updates on individual projects, so there is better transparency. They work on scheduling and expectations, as well as rules of engagement so each team can support the other, as it is the business's responsibility to resource appropriately to support both internal and external customers.

By investing the time to observe how his people were interacting with touchpoints through the business, Henry was able to spot where there were challenges that may have become risks to the business. What seemed to be an insignificant issue at first could have become costly in reputation, revenue and risk. But by being proactive and investing a little time, Henry identified the source of the issue and rectified

> it quickly, without the need to single out a person unfairly. Business requires a team game where you need everyone engaged and connected to succeed or fail... *together.*

Insights: People

- Understand all of the 'touchpoints' each employee has in his or her job and identify frictions that may arise from them.

- Work towards creating a 'Safe Zone' and encourage feedback and communication on processes and tools, so you will hear about areas that are becoming challenges or potential risks.

- Monitor employee engagement levels through activities like relevant and meaningful surveys – if scores are low, find out why.

- Address problematic workplace issues and behaviour, especially at the leadership level, as it's important to lead by example.

Risk Lens

In Chapter 3, we explored harm through the Risk Lens, which looks at risk *to* a person and risk *by* a person. This harm can be physical, emotional or psychological. Increasingly, in the workplace, it takes the form of mental health impact, which can be significant. In 2020, KPMG and the Financial Services Council found that mental health claims had doubled since 2015, and mental illness is now the third most common disability income claim, just behind accidents.[26]

Turning the dial to PROactive

Let's now focus on the importance of viewing an employee's 'touchpoints' through both sides of the Risk Lens. Many large organisations already use processes to identify touchpoints of risk *to* a person. But it is rare for these organisations to drill deeper to identify the risk *by* a person, where the organisation may inadvertently be exposed to risk. This could involve malicious damage, but it may not. Most insider threat incidents are unintentional. In fact, Ponemon has found that two out of three insider threats (63%) are caused by user negligence.[27]

Sometimes these threats arise from people trying to make efficiencies in the process. I have seen many times that if a process is difficult to follow or there are bottlenecks, people can get somewhat creative in finding a way to get their job done, such as skipping steps or ignoring safety precautions. This is especially true when their KPIs are aligned to remuneration-based outcomes, not necessarily how they get them. While we definitely want to encourage innovative thinking, going outside an approved process can open an organisation to risk.

The Risk Lens offers the chance to be proactive around identifying risk. Instead of waiting for an incident to happen that causes harm and then reacting to it, this approach gives you the opportunity to consider the risk to your team much earlier in the process.

CASE STUDY: Peppermint Designs

Peppermint Designs [not its real name] is a clothing designer that has been a huge success, expanding in just two years from selling in one store to supplying a number of retail outlets, and from a team of five to a team of fifty. The company keep a record of all their customer details, previous sales and any customer correspondence in their CRM software. In the early days, when there were only five people in the company, Jules was the entire marketing department, responsible for everything relating to customer relationships. These days, Jules has a team of six people working for her, while some of her old responsibilities have been transferred to newly created teams, including Sales, Finance and Human Resources.

All of these teams use the CRM software for different purposes, and as the company expands new recruits to these departments, they are given logins to access the information. Since a number of different people have taken on different parts of what was once Jules' role, they've all been given the same login profile that she has always used. The trouble is, not everyone requires access to every piece of customer information that's kept in the database – and this poses a risk to

---

Peppermint, its employees and customers. Let's take a look through the Risk Lens.

There is risk *to* the employees because the customer information includes personal details, which carry regulatory and legal obligations, for example those set out by the Privacy Act. Also, the more information each employee can access, the more potential there is for them to make a costly mistake, such as accidentally deleting something. This adds a layer of stress to their working life.

There is also risk *by* the employees. First, someone could make an error. For example, a sales agent contacting a new retailer might accidentally attach the wrong PDF from a customer's file, perhaps details of a negotiated discount rather than a design brochure. Second, a disgruntled employee could access information that could harm the company, for example records of the most popular designs and a full list of customer details, which they might take to a competitor.

Peppermint should introduce different user access profiles so each employee can access only the information they actually need for their role. This will also reduce the temptation for employees to use information for purposes outside the requirements of their roles.

Insights: Risk Lens

- Align KPIs and remuneration packages to make them more realistic. They should not only focus on target outcomes, but also measure how you want the outcome to be achieved (ie by following the correct process).

- Work with all stakeholders to ensure processes do not impede job functions.

- Consider threats posed by all your employees, and extend your analysis to your vendors, stakeholders and customers.

- Consider the people-based risks throughout the entire employee lifecycle.

Origin (of risk)

The origin of risk centres on a person. That is why you need to take a holistic approach to understanding what makes a person tick – their 'risk cocktail' – which we also explored in Chapter 3. There, we took a close look at the four components of the Risk Model – predisposition, stressors, trigger and onset – which play out like a game of Russian Roulette, as we saw in Chapter 4. When you understand the ways these four components operate on people in your organisation, you have the opportunity to turn the dial from a reactive approach to risk, through proactive to predictive, and, better yet, preventative. To get there, you must be genuinely willing to invest the time to get to know your people personally.

Turning the dial towards PROactive

You can view risk to your organisation as simply the gap between understanding potential threats or vulnerabilities and preventing them. As risk starts and ends with people, preventing risk means understanding your people's motivations, ambitions and values, and building a connection with them.

This connection could be built from a common goal, which could be part of the organisation's mission statement. There are many people who seek work in organisations because they believe in its higher purpose (for example, conservation or charity), or mission (such as providing education or healthcare). Even if their role is not intrinsic to this purpose – perhaps they are an accountant, an administrator or a cleaner – they feel their work makes a key contribution to it. For these people, work is more than a pay cheque. There are of course others who are mainly motivated by money, and these people still add considerable value. But it is interesting that the Beaumont Meaningful Work Insights 2019 study noted that only 4% of Australians rated money as the most important thing to them, while 98% agreed that having meaningful work is important.[28] Similarly, *Human Resources Director* reported, 'We have seen the dial shift where workplace culture and meaningful work rather than salary are becoming determining factors for career choices.'[29]

Establishing a deeper connection with your people rewards you with potential productivity improvements and innovation, as they are motivated to make a difference. Research backs this up – well-run organisations with a clear understanding of their internal talent adapt and thrive better than their competitors.[30] One of the best moments for aligning your team's motivation with your organisation's motivations is at the point of recruitment. If you have a values-driven workplace, it will be enhanced by recruiting people who share those values, because they will be motivated by more than just a pay cheque.

CASE STUDY: TravelCover

TravelCover [not its real name] is an insurance agency that specialises in travel insurance. The company was hiring a legal advisor and shortlisted three applicants. Two candidates were experienced lawyers, but not keen travellers, while the third had slightly less legal experience but was an intrepid traveller. Travel was not a requirement of the role, but the recruitment team decided to hire the third candidate. His eyes lit up when he talked about his adventures and he had called on his travel insurance policy a number of times to get him out sticky situations overseas. The team felt that he brought an understanding of their clients and a passion for assisting them to the role that was even more valuable than extra legal experience.

Insights: Origin

- Leverage the four components of the Risk Model to turn the dial from reactive to proactive and, in time, to preventative.

- Maximise internal teams, trusted external partners, knowledge processes and tools to support a person-centred risk program.

- Implement employee support programs (employee assistance programs, harassment officers and mental health first aid) to improve stress management.

- Implement leadership programs and encourage managers to develop self-awareness, ethical intelligence and leadership skills.

Summary

At first, it is not easy to train your focus on people as the first consideration in mitigating risk. Organisations are usually looking for ways to reduce costs while finding efficiencies, so yes, systems and technologies are appealing. But don't lose sight of the value and opportunities that people hold. Relying heavily on systems and technology can bring short-term gains, but some can end up being band-aids – superficial solutions that not only impact negatively on employees but the organisation as a whole. Remember that business also starts and ends with people, so take a balanced approach that enables you to focus on your core business.

When exploring risk in your organisation, keep in mind it is not just about aiming to mitigate the risk, but exploring what opportunities there are. Risk is at the core of my business, yet every time we go deeper into an organisation's risk profile, we find opportunity, sometimes great opportunity. There is reward in risk, though it may require a more in-depth journey (and greater commitment, trust and focus on its people).

In the next chapter, we'll take a look at the final crucial elements in the PROTECT framework, and the ways you can make tangible changes to protect the house.

8
PROTECT – Step Two

Once you have gained an understanding of people, the way risk operates in relation to them (the Risk Lens), and what makes them tick (the origin of risk), we can look at the other four elements that play a crucial role. Remember the PROTECT framework acronym:

- **P**eople
- **R**isk Lens
- **O**rigin (of Risk)
- **T**rust
- **E**nvironment
- **C**ollaboration
- **T**oolkit

In this chapter, Step Two of the PROTECT framework, we'll look at trust, environment, collaboration and toolkit.

Trust

As we all intuitively know, trust is a feeling – often a gut feeling. It cannot be purchased, outsourced, automated, created through a policy or process, or sent out as a message. Trust is an emotion, as it relates to the limbic system, which is involved in motivation, emotion, learning and memory. It is also worth noting the limbic system is responsible for loyalty. Emotions are tied to our daily choices, so respecting and valuing them is important.

What reaction do you have when you hear the word 'trust'? Is it a positive, warm feeling? Or are you in the other camp, like many people we have spoken with, where you feel the word 'trust' has become a commodity. It no longer holds the same value as it used to because of the perceived abuse of the word in marketing campaigns and throwaway lines from people and organisations that are happy to promote trust but aren't actually earning it.

In his book, *The Thin Book of Trust*, Charles Feltman defines trust as 'choosing to risk making something you value vulnerable to another person's actions'. Feltman writes about the potential value created through trust, but how 'good work is being sabotaged by interpersonal conflict, political infighting, paralysis, stagnation, apathy, or cynicism.'[31]

A key problem we have come across is when an organisation's leadership expects trust from their employees without first proving themselves to be trustworthy. When employees hear their organisation promoting itself as transparent, collegial or supportive, when their lived experience of it is different, they feel that their organisation is simply paying lip service to these values, or worse, trying to manipulate them. This can lead to distrust and suspicion, then to disengagement and disgruntlement, all of which pose a risk to your organisation.

Turning the dial towards PROactive

There are so many formulas or checklists for building trust, but even if you theoretically follow all the right steps, you can still get it wrong. So how do you create trust? Stephen MR Covey, author of the book *The Speed of Trust*, challenges the assumption that trust is a social virtue, asserting that it is actually a hard-edge economic driver – that is, a learnable and measurable skill. Stephen's father, Stephen M Covey, author of *The 7 Habits of Highly Effective People* agrees and shared that when his son took over the business, Covey Leadership Center, using the very principles he had shared in *The Speed of Trust*, within three years, sales had doubled, profit went up over 1,200%, and shareholder value increased from $2.4 million to $160 million.[32] His trust principles were key to this success.

So trust can be built through a process, even though it is an emotion. A Griffith University study in 2018 found that the second-strongest influence on employee job satisfaction in Australia was management's trust and empowerment – in other words, if you want satisfied employees, you must demonstrate your confidence or trust in them.[33] Using a structured, even tick-box approach and process can absolutely help you do this, especially when it comes from a sincere desire to build trust.

Keep in mind that trust is something given and by building a pathway to a person, they may feel safe to walk that pathway and trust you. There are, however, organisations who expect loyalty and trust from their employees while sending clear signals that they don't trust their employees in return, for example, by imposing onerous systems, checks and approval processes. There have been cases where employees have interpreted such systems as an implication that they are negligent or incompetent, or worse, that management feel they have malicious intent.

Let me ask you something – the last time someone gave you misinformation, misled you, withheld important information that impacted your decisions or second-guessed everything you did, did you continue to trust them?

CASE STUDY: Salesforce

Salesforce have been on the 'Fortune 100 Best Companies to Work For' list for twelve years running, and in 2018, they hit number one on the list. How do they do it? According to the company's blog, 'At Salesforce, we believe nothing is more important than our people. We are an Ohana – the Hawaiian word for family – that includes our customers, employees, partners, and communities.'[34] A culture of trust is central to everything they do.

Fortune 100's list shows that it's the companies that employees say are great workplaces that demonstrate stronger financial performance, reduced staff turnover, and better customer and patient satisfaction than their peers.[35]

Insights: Trust

Below are some ways to foster confidence and trust, but remember: trust is a feeling, not just a box that can be ticked – you can use a process to help build a strong bridge that people feel safe to cross.

- Develop communication skills, especially clarity, consistency and transparency.

- Implement cultural change at the leadership level – share it, act it, do it.

- Develop a value-based framework and deliver values training.

- Build skills for confidence, with programs like conflict resolution, tactical empathy programs, diversity programs and emotional intelligence.

Environment

While leaders cannot directly control the degree of confidence or trust employees place in the organisation, they do have control over a major determining factor: the work environment.

As we saw in Chapter 6, the only way to create an environment where people feel safe to succeed is to make a space where people feel safe to make mistakes or even fail – the Safe Zone. Here, people are looking out for one another. There are no scapegoats, there's no blame-shifting and no one gets thrown under the bus. According to *Harvard Business Review* leadership analyst Roger Jones, 'CEOs should actively encourage all team members to speak up without fear of consequences. That fosters honesty, debate and better decisions.'[36]

In some work environments, there's a problem with prioritising systems over people. Technology writer Vala Afshar points to the example of the introduction of Information Technology in the workplace. It began in the 1950s, when companies invested heavily in a large, expensive and complicated new technology: computers. They realised they needed to protect their new investment, and the nascent IT departments were tasked with just one job: to protect the computers and ensure they were used as efficiently as possible. Innovation and customer service were not part of their job description. This introduced a 'systems before people' mentality that still dominates thinking in many IT teams.[37] It is not only unhelpful for innovation but is outdated in its thinking.

For full disclosure, I personally love innovative and cutting-edge technologies. They are part of my toolkit, but they must work well for people and for the business. And keep in mind that some skilled people, when disgruntled, can use your systems and technology as a weapon against you. Look after your people first.

Turning the dial towards PROactive

When things go wrong in a work environment, a number of issues could be contributing, for example, the wrong policies could be in place, or ineffective process. Perhaps someone needs a bit more training in leadership or communication skills. It could be that the leadership team is having trouble just making a decision and committing to it unanimously.

These are not ground-breaking concepts, but the reward in addressing them is a reduction in your organisation's risk profile.

CASE STUDY: Carrama

Carrama [not its real name] is a finance consultancy that is having trouble defining its KPIs for its latest strategic plan. One member of the senior executive attends a workshop on a new KPI process and recommends it to the rest of the executive.

Most of the executive finds the system reasonable, if not compelling. But one member of the executive, Harry, really doesn't buy it. He's used a similar system in a previous role and he believes it adds to the administrative burden without bringing any real results. Harry argues against the new system but the executive decides to give it a try.

Harry is frustrated. He feels the rest of the group failed to listen to him and take his experience into account. The executive agrees to a compromise and because of his reservations, Harry's team does not take part in using the new system. But the model relies on information and responses to be shared between teams, so those who work with Harry's team are not able to collect all the information they need. They're disadvantaged in the KPI measures, which have been linked to remuneration. Tensions start to build as Harry's team becomes the target of frustration from other teams. It's a mess.

How could this have been avoided? Cohesiveness around executive decisions is critical. In an environment of doubt and indecision, the Carrama employees can't be expected to perform at their best. There needs to be a decision-making process that ensures all executives are heard and understood, but when a decision is made, regardless of any one person's bias or preference, there is a commitment from the executive team to engage with and execute the decision fully. In this instance, Harry could have provided useful insights from his past experience, but needed to set his own agenda or bias aside to abide by the executive team's decision once it had been made. If this couldn't be done, the executive should have considered abandoning the idea.

You can't begin a sweeping new strategy without the full commitment of the entire leadership team. Personal agendas and biases can create risk to an organisation. All roads and decisions should lead back to the right decision for the business, not just one person. Focusing on the brand, its values, mission and objectives to underpin decisions can help executive teams remain focused on the business in their deliberations.

Insights: Environment

- Connect with your people – this is critical for building a strong culture. Ensure that your messaging addresses your current culture and your destination if your organisation is transitioning.

- Ensure reviews of operational processes are relevant and up to date, but also consistent with policy.

- Create a Safe Zone in your organisation by making it safe to fail, as well as safe to succeed, and supporting people with training wheels.

- Create a team of executive leaders that your employees deserve – think about what it would be like to have the type of leader you wish you had and give that opportunity to your people.

Collaboration

Collaboration excites me as a person. I'm drawn to working with others with a common goal or objective and relish the opportunity to maximise the strength, skills, insights and knowledge of a focused collective, one that surpasses what we could have delivered as individuals.

But many people don't collaborate well, often from fear of not wanting to share 'valuable' information, of rejection, of being seen as a weak contributor, of feeling vulnerable, or of exposing their limitations, because the culture is aggressively competitive. This creates a barrier to learning about better practices. Limited knowledge and skillsets create silos in the workplace, information blocks and knowledge gaps, and turning inwards, rather than collaborating, is one of the shortest routes to organisational limitation, and for some, even demise. It's far better to take an expansive approach, even at the risk of exposing vulnerabilities. As Henry Ford stated, 'Coming together is a beginning; keeping together is progress; working together is success',[38] or as Thomas Stallkamp put it, 'The secret is to gang up on the problem, rather than each other.'[39]

Turning the dial towards PROactive

At its best, effective collaborations harness the strengths of each person, and compensate for perceived areas of weakness or bias. This requires a level of openness from you to discuss those vulnerabilities with your collaborators. If you operate from only one perspective, you will always be limited by your own biases, which can prove dangerous.

To undertake genuine collaboration, there must be a concerted effort to reach out and be open to learning from others. Identify internal or external individuals and groups that have the skills, knowledge and tools to fill organisational limitations or gaps, or who will inject a different perspective. Be clear on the objectives and keep the need to do what's right for the organisation at the forefront. Also keep in mind that there will be blind spots, especially when personal bias or ego comes into play. Setting rules of engagement, or even bringing in a facilitator might help you improve collaborative efforts if this is a challenge.

When you get collaboration right, whether it is through partnerships or by accessing the untapped skills of people already in your organisation, you will benefit from an expanded knowledge base, toolkit, skillset and analytic framework.

CASE STUDY: Intexton

Intexton [not its real name] provides bespoke technology solutions to education providers. One of its most important clients, a large university department, has experienced problems with the student portal developed by Intexton. The account manager, Meilei, meets with the university administrator, Sandra, who stresses that the problem must be fixed urgently, before term starts. Meilei promises that the problem will be fixed as early as possible, but Sandra presses her for a deadline date. Meilei, whose background is in sales, not software development, relies on the standard timeframe she's been given for fixing portal issues. 'We'll have this fixed in two weeks,' she promises.

Back at Intexton, Meilei tells Cameron, the head of the development team, that they have two weeks to fix the issue. Cameron is appalled – this is a complex issue and will take at least four weeks to fix. Meilei points out that Cameron has previously given her a two-week timeframe for portal issues. He explains to Meilei that this is not a standard portal issue.

The university is an important client and the executive director steps into the dispute. He feels that they've already made the commitment to the customer, and they'll need to find some way to meet the deliverables negotiated by Meilei. Cameron's team ends up working through the night to put the fix in place. Everyone,

---

including Meilei, Cameron, the executive director and especially Cameron's team, are frustrated and disgruntled. They miss the deadline and Sandra is not impressed.

How could this have been avoided? Meilei did not have the technical skills to put a timeframe on fixing the issue, while Cameron did not have a relationship with the client to negotiate the arrangements. A better solution would have been for both Meilei and Cameron to attend the meeting with the client. Alternatively, Intexton should develop a standard policy to provide resolution timeframes to clients within twenty-four hours, rather than on the spot, to give the development team a chance to assess the issue.

Insights: Collaboration

- Learn more about your own biases through training in cognitive bias and unconscious bias programs.

- Invest in communication, conflict resolution and networking skills.

- Identify effective facilitators or mediators to enhance collaborative efforts.

- Use collaborative, multiple-criteria decision-making processes.

Toolkit

We have reached the final 'T' in the PROTECT framework – toolkit – and this is where you should be considering all the resources (tools) you have at your disposal. This includes all of your people, their skills and knowledge, your processes, systems and technology capabilities, and all the other resources that you put to use in your business.

When the topic of the organisation's toolkit is raised, our clients' focus often turns to systems and technology solutions. This is understandable – with today's rapid advances in technology, newer and shinier solutions to problems are available each year. Organisations are looking for ways to scale and reduce costs, which is why so many are turning to newer technology. But could this be adding more risk to your organisational profile? Unfortunately, an exclusive focus on systems and technologies can mean that people aren't being considered in the way they should be.

It is hard not to be drawn in by the advancements taking place in technology. The artificial intelligence (AI) market is expected to reach USD $190.61 billion by 2025.[40] But it's likely to be some time before we can trust software to fully protect us.[41] As UK-based information security evangelist Del Aden has remarked, 'AI has made the challenge both more addressable and more of a risk.'[42] He points to some of the many ethical concerns that have cropped up since the widespread use of AI has begun to impact real people's lives, such as in racial profiling and consumer rights infringements.

No tool is a silver bullet. As AI pioneer Dr Maria Milosavljevic has said, 'Technology has gone a bit too far. We've lost the balance and we really need to be having more conversations about ethical AI.'[43] Entrepreneurs, scientists and business tycoons like Bill Gates,[44] Elon Musk[45] and Stephen Hawking[46] have expressed caution around AI, often comparing advanced technologies to a double-edged sword.

When it comes to these niche and emerging technologies, I am excited by the possibilities they offer, but remain diligent so I can make an informed decision. When someone asks my opinion, I could speak all day about my thoughts around the pros and cons of such technology, but the main point is that technology should be working for people, not the other way around. Powerful technology capabilities like AI may be a tool of the trade for one person but they can also be purposed as a weapon for someone else. I will share some examples later in the section to provide insights into the benefits and concerns relating to AI. If you are keen to use sophisticated analytics and AI, then do your homework. Books such as *Artificial Intelligence – A Guide for Thinking Humans* by Melanie Mitchell offer a pragmatic approach to understanding the value and risks associated with this technology.[47]

If you implement systems and technology solutions that make the work environment difficult for people to navigate, you will impede your employees which, in turn, impedes your business. Organisations today must comply with some level of legal, policy and governance requirements, and processes, policies, systems and technology can facilitate this. But it's worth pausing to consider the potential impact on your most valuable asset – your people.

Turning the dial towards PROactive

Any new tool should be put through a sanity check. As we discussed under the Risk Lens, you should look through the person's perspective. In the case of a new technology capability, perhaps start with the employees expected to use the tool, then move to the processes and systems involved in the use of the technology. At each stage, you should validate the feasibility of what you are doing and examine the impact on the whole business, not just the benefits for one department.

There are technologies you might be implementing to aid your understanding of your organisation's risk profile. As risk starts and ends with people, employee monitoring capabilities might be of interest to you, though it's worth conducting a thorough analysis of the impact of these technologies on your people. In some cases, you may discover they create stressors that could lead to increased risks.

To turn risk into opportunity, you need to consider questions like:

- What impact does the tool have on all current and future touchpoints and interactions?

- Is the organisation looking in a holistic manner to maximise the value to the business? Or is the tool being delivered in a disjointed or piecemeal manner?

- Is the tool causing conflict between different parts of the organisation?

- Are two parts of the organisation replicating the same tool?

It pays to keep the same principles in mind when implementing any tool that influences your people, including policies. Often the driver for a policy comes from areas like governance or legal, which means they can be dry and dense in how they are written and the responsibilities communicated. These policies can also create obstacles for employees through restriction and additional rigour. If these measures are necessary, ensure the employee's expectations align with the restrictions or additional workload being created, and the employee is not being penalised.

Creating a safe and fair work environment is critical, as is setting your people up for success. Remember, there is reward in the right type of effort, so look to your people in the process and always look after your people.

Now, as promised, I will share some case studies relating to AI. There is definitely exciting potential with such technological ventures, but as I mentioned earlier, there are also risks.

CASE STUDIES:
AI

Exciting developments in healthcare

Within the healthcare industry, AI is kicking many goals. The pharmaceutical industry and research institutions are using AI to support budgeting and the generation of better drugs. Microsoft's Hanover uses AI to help determine which drug combinations are the most effective for a cancer patient.[48] Medical image analysis is being supported with AI to assist with image quality. Improvements in areas like ultrasounds and MRI help analyse tissues in much less time. Advances in automated image diagnosis are also helping to improve service and response time.

AI assistance in healthcare has been growing over the years with robot-assisted surgeries, virtual nursing assistance, clinical trial participant identifiers, and preliminary diagnosis, to touch on just a handful of examples.[49]

Healthcare is often burdened by limitations in resources and AI has the potential to support hospitals,

---

clinics and workers to provide better care at scale. It is an exciting example of where improvements are being used to support people's well-being.

Risks and challenges of AI

But AI also presents risks, even for large, tech-savvy companies. Amazon had to hit the pause button on providing their facial recognition software, known as Rekognition, to certain US law enforcement agencies due to the number of misclassification errors and algorithmic biases found in the software.[50]

AI can be powerful in helping us to explore data, but when it comes to critical decisions, we are still accountable for the outcomes. Such an example is the Uber self-driving car that tragically killed a pedestrian in Tempe, Arizona, USA in 2018. The back-up driver was charged with negligent homicide. The limitation of the technology in this case was discovered in the worst way, where it takes a life instead of providing protection.

At a time where the confidence in autonomous vehicle technology had grown to an all-time high, the outcome of this incident sent shockwaves and saw testing programmes by rivals like Google's Waymo and Chinese tech Baidu pushed back.[51]

Artificial Intelligence can be weaponised

When is your voice not your voice? When you have been caught out in a voice-spoofing attack. A UK-based energy firm found out the hard way, when the CEO of the company believed he was on a call with his boss, the chief executive of the firm's German parent company, and followed instructions to immediately transfer €220,000 (approx. AUD $340,000) to the bank account of a Hungarian supplier.[52]

That voice actually belonged to a fraudster leveraging AI voice technology to spoof the CEO. The firm's insurance company shared that the fraudster called the company three times: the first to initiate the transfer, the second to falsely claim it had been reimbursed, and a third time seeking a follow-up payment. The victim grew sceptical by the third time, but the first payment had already been cleared and finalised.

Another example that became a valuable lesson involved the release of Microsoft's AI chatbot Tay.[53] The chatbot was designed to develop conversational understanding as it interacted with people through social media. However, within twenty-four hours, malicious Twitter users had attacked and exploited a vulnerability through the human interaction and learning process, causing the bot to respond to tweets with a series of lewd and racist tweets. Microsoft had to apologise for the unintended offensive and hurtful posts from Tay. It was a huge lesson that sophisticated technology can be weaponised quickly.

Do your due diligence

The advancements in specialised technologies like AI have the potential to offer exciting opportunities in many facets of business and life, especially in areas like medical and healthcare services. There are many positive initiatives taking place across all sectors, but the purpose of the case studies presented here is to highlight that even though we have come so far, there is still much work to be done.

Investing the time to do your due diligence is critically important. Don't get caught up in the product marketing. Make sure you identify the vulnerabilities and threats, the ethical considerations, not to mention the limitations of the technology capabilities you are exploring so you can truly make an informed decision. There is no silver bullet in technology, and there are also risks. But without a doubt, there can be many benefits. And please remind yourself that technology should be a tool that works for people first.

Insights: Toolkit

- Conduct due diligence and pragmatic sanity checks on any new tool.

- Follow the thread of the touchpoints, keeping in mind people, processes and policies, systems and technology.

- If the new tool has the potential to change or impede an employee's ability to perform their work, ensure their expected deliverables and KPIs are also adjusted and in line with what is reasonably possible.

- Implement clear and consistent policies.

Summary

The PROTECT framework establishes the seven elements of people-centred risk protection. By implementing the actions outlined in Chapters 7 and 8, you can transform your risk profile and create a positive workplace culture where employees feel motivated to protect your organisation from risk.

The PROTECT framework provides a clear method for putting people back into the centre of your business while also addressing risk management. It is a tool for organisations to turn risk into reward and start reaping the many benefits you gain when you protect the house.

9
Dave's Dilemma:
A Case Study

The PROTECT framework is a powerful tool to reorient your thinking around risk, and sometimes it's easier to visualise the process with an example. In this chapter, we'll take a look at Dave's story. Dave is a fictional character but I'm pretty sure you'll recognise him straight away, especially if you've spent any time working in a large organisation.

Spoiler alert: Dave's story does not have a happy ending. But taking a close look at the moments where the story turns from bad to worse can give us enormous insight into how we can avoid making the same mistakes ourselves.

Dave's story

Meet Dave, a thirty-something professional who has just seen an interesting job advertisement for a large global organisation. The ad promotes an inclusive work culture and mentions that high value is placed on nurturing key talent. Dave is proud of his impressive track record of overdelivering on targets and he sees the opportunity to work with a team of similarly high-achieving colleagues. The remuneration package appears attractive too.

The eager new recruit

Dave applies for the job and lands it. He is excited as his boss, Kate, welcomes him on board, explaining the generous performance incentives on offer. Dave is energised and can't wait to get to work and prove himself as a performer.

But Dave can't get to work straight away. The onboarding is intense – there's a week of training to understand systems, record-keeping and security provisions. Dave feels overwhelmed but he does his best to take in the requirements.

Eventually Dave starts his job and is eager to create a good impression. In the beginning, he tries to navigate the processes as he's been taught, but he finds himself running into obstacles. He relies on other departments for sign-offs on certain tasks and he finds that bottlenecks appear. Some of his projects almost grind to a halt as he faithfully waits for inputs, such as credit vetting and validation of a number of customers' personal details.

Missing targets

Dave is struggling with internal challenges. He becomes stressed and starts to feel demoralised as he has always thought of himself as an achiever, an outcomes guy. He now realises that he will not be able to meet his KPIs or hit his target earnings, as these are linked to his KPIs. Meanwhile, Dave's peers don't seem to be having any trouble – in fact, some are smashing their KPI targets.

Dave does not want to let Kate know he's struggling. Instead, he turns to one of his colleagues in the team, Tim, and asks him out for lunch to get the inside scoop. Dave quizzes Tim cautiously (he doesn't want to appear incompetent) about his ways of getting around the bottlenecks.

Tim is surprised that Dave is waiting for clearance before setting up an account and order for customers, and following the other official processes. There is just too much red tape, Tim remarks. No one actually goes through the motions of the 'correct procedure' outlined during induction. How would they ever meet their targets doing that?

Tim explains the way everyone else navigates the obstacles to get the work done. For example, they use access rights to one of the systems used by the vetting teams, shared by former team member, Heidi, whose credentials remain active. Everyone just uses Heidi's details and logs in to tick the 'vetting completed' box. Dave is surprised – it was stressed during his training that he must follow procedure and do the vetting through the official channels. But Tim reassures Dave that no one waits for clearance, or they would simply never meet their KPIs. The KPIs are more important than the procedure. 'We just need to be a little creative around how we get there,' says Tim. 'Kate turns a blind eye.'

The short cut to success

Dave feels unsettled and nervous about trying Tim's approach. He fears a reprimand or backlash. But his performance is stagnating and he wants to keep his personal reputation as a doer. Dave tries Tim's process – he uses Heidi's login details to access one of his customer's submissions and, with a couple clicks of the mouse, completes the authorisation of the customer account and order without the appropriate authorisation. He braces himself for repercussions – a complaint, an alarm or a reprimand – but there appears to be no harm done. Dave adopts more of Tim's 'creative' suggestions. Suddenly, he is smashing his KPIs and his earnings increase dramatically.

Dave begins to use Tim's processes without thinking twice and finds even more efficiencies as he reaches out to other colleagues to learn their 'creative' work-arounds. He justifies his decision to cut corners by telling himself it's the organisation's responsibility to sort out inefficient processes. In any case, everyone is doing the same thing. Dave's KPIs are only related to the outcome, not the process – so this is clearly the priority for the business.

Dave begins to kick goals at work. He even wins a couple of performance awards over the next eighteen months.

The restructure

Then the organisation goes through a restructure. Jobs are cut, new teams are formed, others are blended. Each employee must apply for one of the new roles. Dave has worked hard and really delivered for the business, but the process of reapplying for a role leaves him feeling unappreciated.

It seems like the organisation does not value its people and is more focused on reducing operational costs. He hears a rumour that the business is also planning to weed out people who don't meet some new criteria, but no one knows what these mysterious criteria are.

The new manager

Dave keeps his role, but a few of his colleagues do not, including Tim and Kate. He has a new manager, Bruce, who comes from a competing organisation. Bruce organises refresher training and underlines the processes the team needs to follow in their roles. The training and official processes re-emphasise the things Dave learned back in induction – like the need for credit vetting and validation of clients. Dave doesn't even consider complying, he knows that stuff is all hot air. He continues to use the processes that have helped him hit his targets and win his awards.

The tip-off

Bruce starts poking into records that Dave did not even know existed. Bruce begins running reports and system alerts based on his list of direct reports, which for this organisation, means current and past employees of this team. Bruce notices Heidi's access credentials being used to access systems that are not required or authorised. Bruce starts his own investigation to understand what is happening. Soon enough, he learns about the access credentials and speaks to each member of his team. Bruce asks Dave why he accessed records directly, rather than following the official process to obtain permission. Dave explains that what he has been doing is standard practice within the team and he was introduced to this approach soon after he started.

Bruce shares with Dave that the senior executive had sensed there were some dangerous practices going on within the division, such as breaching legislative privacy obligations and fraudulent activities. Bruce confides that he has been brought in to identify and resolve them.

The wake-up call

Dave is shocked. This has never come up before. Kate was only interested in hitting the targets – she didn't care how the team went about getting there because her superiors, in turn, were also only interested in outcomes. Dave is now on notice and he fears that he is being watched and judged. He tries to implement the official processes, but sure enough, his productivity plummets. He can't get clearance and authorisation to credit vetting and validation of personal information fast enough and his opportunities go cold. His fear quickly gives way to frustration. How can he be expected to meet his KPIs when he must wait weeks for a rubber stamp just to carry out his job? Dave feels that the organisation should fix the process if they expect him to deliver the targets they've set.

He raises the issue with Bruce, and demands Bruce fix the bottleneck. But credit vetting and validation of personal information is managed by another team. Bruce raises it with the other team's manager and they make some improvements – setting up a priority clearance system – but it only knocks a week off the waiting time. There's no way it will enable Dave and his team to perform at their previous levels.

The tightening screws

Cracks start to appear. Dave's team find solace in one another, taking turns to raise their frustrations with Bruce. They quickly harden in their attitude against the new boss. Bruce decides to make an example of a couple of team members. He puts someone on a Performance Improvement Plan (PIP) and dismisses another for policy breaches. Bruce hopes the fear of dismissal will bring the rest of the team into line.

But the opposite occurs. The team feel they have been treated badly by the organisation and by their new manager, after many years of impressive performance for the business. They become angry and disengaged and Bruce notices everyone is making more errors.

The calm response

But Dave takes a different approach. He conceals his frustration and goes through the motions of doing his job. From Bruce's perspective, he is complying and trying to improve. Even though his results are terrible, he is faithfully following the process.

Bruce focuses on managing the performance of the noise-makers, going where he believes his immediate attention is required. He leaves others, including Dave – who is concealing his true feelings – alone, even though their performance is poor. Sensing resistance from his team, Bruce starts to appoint new members to the team and fill some of the vacated roles. This makes Dave and his colleagues frustrated and resentful, because the new recruits are bubbly and eager and they don't feel the injustices felt by the existing team.

Dave, meanwhile, has been actively looking for another job. He has been taking longer lunch breaks, using doctor's appointments or compassionate leave to go to interviews, and his performance drops even further. Bruce calls Dave on this, and Dave begins to fear he will put him on a PIP. Dave does not want a PIP against his name while he's looking for a new job. So Dave searches with more urgency, which in turn impacts his productivity even more.

The Performance Improvement Plan

One day, Bruce sits Dave down and says his performance has fallen to a critical level – the next step will be a PIP. Dave's worst fear is being realised. Dave remains calm, again concealing his true emotions and frustration. He says the issue is with the organisation, that the organisation needs to fix the bottleneck. Bruce says he appreciates the feedback, but that doesn't change Dave's poor performance.

Dave feels victimised. He's had enough. He begins plotting his exit even as Bruce talks him through the next steps. Dave walks out of Bruce's office with next steps of his own. Over the following few days, he discreetly makes a copy of his customer contact list and key process documents, planning to use these when he goes to a competitor.

The new job

During the next week, Dave accepts a new job. It's not his dream job, but he has to get out of the organisation before he has the black mark of a PIP against his name. Dave remains calm when he hands Bruce his letter of resignation, explaining that he is going to a competitor. Dave knows this will instantly put him on gardening leave, where he will exit the business that day, without returning to his computer. But this is no problem – he has already taken the information he wants. Dave remains calm and compliant, so for Bruce, there are no alarm bells. They only go off a few months later when it becomes evident that Dave has been poaching clients and using information from the organisation to benefit the competitor company.

A new narrative: Using the PROTECT framework

Many of us are familiar with stories just like Dave's. Perhaps we know a Dave or we've even been Dave at one time or another. At first, this story can seem like an inevitable tragedy – after all, there's no one person who is to blame, no villain in the story. But when we begin to analyse Dave's story through the PROTECT framework, we can see that there are many moments when a well-timed intervention might have resulted in a different outcome.

People

Dave was expected to deliver on tough KPIs, which impacted his remuneration. But the operational measures were so restrictive that he actually could not meet his targets by following the official procedure. Restricting employees and penalising them through their KPIs is never a good mix. Dave's first manager, Kate, turned a blind eye to the short cuts her employees were taking, because she too was being held to outcome-based KPIs.

When Bruce came on board, his objective was different and the parameters changed. But instead of engaging with Dave to learn about the frustrations and roadblocks he encountered while trying to fulfil his role, Bruce doubled down on the tight process and restrictions.

If Dave's workplace had created a Safe Zone, he may have felt comfortable raising his initial discomfort about the disconnect between the official procedure and the creative workaround with his first boss, Kate.

When he raised it with Bruce, his concerns were disregarded and he was about to be put on a PIP. Bruce could have devoted some time and resources to investigating the team's challenges and touchpoints, since Dave and his team were vocalising the same issues.

Risk Lens

The risk *to* Dave came from the restrictions he faced in performing his job function, which caused him stress. When Bruce applied pressure and made Dave accountable for following formal processes, he was no longer able to cut corners. Dave had become disengaged and when he was threatened with a PIP, he panicked.

Let's note here that there was also risk *to* Dave by having the option to use Heidi's login credentials. Access should have been deactivated when the employee left the organisation. This inaction by the organisation actually transitioned a risk *to* Dave (the temptation to use the details) into a risk *by* Dave and other team members as they used the credentials to interact with systems and processes where they were not authorised to be, which exposed the organisation.

When Bruce came on board, the team dynamics changed. Dave and other members of the team became disengaged and their productivity dropped as they were not paying attention to details – nor did they care that they had to – representing risk *by* Dave and the team.

If Kate or Bruce had taken a look at Dave's situation through the Risk Lens, they would have quickly seen that he was under pressure. If either had invested the time to follow Dave's process and touchpoints through exploring risk *to* a person and risk *by* a person, the causes of bottlenecks could have been identified and resolved earlier.

Origin

The origin of risk takes us back to focusing on the person and what makes them tick, leveraging the four components of the Risk Model – predisposition, stressors, trigger and onset.

Dave's *predisposition* was that he saw himself as a high achiever. He liked to feel valued and respected for performing well. When he was stressed, he did not lash out, and presented little sign of being under pressure. When he did not feel safe, he concealed his feelings and avoided confrontation.

Dave's *stressors* included having to navigate a process that impeded his ability to do his job, fulfil the role and meet his targets. The disruption of the restructure and having to reapply for his role added stress, not to mention the loss of his colleagues, Tim and Kate. Dave had to adapt to a change in management style and try to make sense of the inconsistent views on accountability from each manager. Dave's stress bucket was reaching full capacity.

The *trigger* that caused an onset and led him to change his behaviour was the threat of a Performance Improvement Plan. For a man who was proud of his record as a peak performer to be placed on a PIP was the ultimate insult. It touched on his core values, insecurities and threatened his sense of identity – in other words, it was a stress multiplier.

Dave's *onset* was not expressed outwardly, but concealed. He appeared to be complying with Bruce's instructions, but in reality, he was stealing valuable information in the form of the organisation's customer list and key process documents.

Trust

From the beginning of Dave's journey, his trust in leadership was on a slow decline. Out of his own insecurities, he did not trust Kate enough to confide that he was struggling to meet his KPIs, instead turning to Tim for advice. He saw the shortcomings of the official procedure and did not trust the organisation to deal with them if he provided feedback, so instead he began to take short cuts. When the restructure rolled around, Dave felt management was using it as an excuse to weed out people, and did not feel safe to ask questions about it.

When Dave's new manager Bruce revealed he had been brought in to identify and resolve issues, Dave felt that the organisation had not been open about the reasons behind the change in leadership. By the time Bruce began to use fear tactics, threatening to put people on PIPs, Dave's trust in the organisation had entirely evaporated.

Environment

Dave answered an ad for a company that promoted itself as having an inclusive workplace culture that valued key talent. But when he came on board, he found the real environment to be different. There was a huge mismatch between the official processes he learned during his induction and the actual practices of his team.

When the organisation restructured, the work environment changed in response to a new manager who had different priorities. Dave and his colleagues were left feeling destabilised – as though there was no steady ground on which to stand.

Collaboration

From the start, Dave discovered that his organisation's communication was not consistent, and he was the one who would be held accountable for his own deliverables. When he was first employed, Kate overlooked the unofficial workarounds, while Bruce took a hard line. When Dave raised his observations about the failings in the system with Bruce, there was no noticeable change.

Bruce could have taken a collaborative approach with the line manager of the team responsible for credit vetting and validation of personal information. Together, they could have identified the main causes for the bottleneck and brainstormed appropriate alternatives. If they had no way of resolving the bottleneck, they could have revisited more appropriate KPIs so all employees had the opportunity to succeed within the restrictive working environment.

Toolkit

The toolkit operating in Dave's workplace was not working. For a start, there were stark inconsistencies between policy and practice. Although the organisation had invested in technology to alert managers to breaches in protocols, no action was taken by Kate when the protocols were breached. She knew that actioning the alert would result in a drop in productivity, and this would harm her own KPIs.

If leadership had taken the time to sanity check the processes Dave was expected to use to meet his KPIs, they would have quickly discovered that it was not possible to meet the targets through the official process. Equally, if they had taken the time to consider the restructure from the perspective of the employees, they may have been able to more effectively manage the change and communication associated with it.

Summary

Dave went from eager new recruit to disgruntled and malicious former employee. And yet, this terrible downward spiral that sucked in everyone – Dave, Tim, Kate, Bruce, the organisation and its customers – could have been prevented.

Dave's story has shown us the way in which each element of the PROTECT framework is critical in helping to address risk. His experience was fictional, but stories like this play out time and time again in organisations. In the next chapter, we'll take a look at some of the benefits you gain when instead of spiralling into the Risk Vortex, you learn how to protect the house.

PART 4
FIND REWARD IN RISK

10
Reputation, Revenue And Risk

I want you to imagine your organisation sometime in the future. Every single person in your organisation is invested in its success. People are turning up with their best ideas and solutions. But more than that – your people are so attuned to the needs and sensitivities of the organisation that they aren't just looking at how to help it succeed, but they're also fiercely protective of it. They have become your risk sensors.

Your people are your organisation's greatest asset. Organisations that understand the connection between individual and organisational risk place themselves at a competitive advantage. They benefit not only from reduced risk, increased revenue and improved reputation (the Three Rs), but also from an attractive work environment.[54]

The PROTECT framework presents all the elements you need to put people at the centre of risk, improve your workplace culture and embed corporate social responsibility into your organisation. Once you achieve these, an abundance of benefits flow your way. There is reward in the right type of effort.

In this chapter, we'll take a look at these benefits, along with some examples of how the world's true leaders have achieved them. We'll also examine how leaders have connected people through a purpose.

Reputation

The reputation of your organisation is carried by multiple channels, including media advertising, word of mouth, communication from your executives and your people, and every other touchpoint you have with customers and the community. All these channels influence the way you are perceived by people and can provide a competitive advantage.

The power of people

Connecting with people, ensuring their safety and providing a workplace that is a 'safe to succeed' environment, enables employees to feel valued for their contributions. This, in turn, creates a reputation for integrity and fair dealing – if your employees are proud to work for you, then your customers will benefit. Trustworthiness spreads from inside the workplace out into the marketplace. All stakeholders put their faith – and their money – in the organisation's products or services. Engagement and investment in the organisation is high.

If you take care of your people, they will be motivated and empowered to take care of your customers – happy employees offer better service. This is not new. Richard Branson has always championed the idea of putting employees first. His overall maxim is, 'Staff first, customers second, and shareholders third.'[55]

Example: Richard Branson

Richard Branson is one of the world's most inspiring leaders. *Industry Leaders* magazine summed up his achievements as, 'a remarkable leader with soaring desire to kindle the moral fibre of leadership in many lives, chairman of over 400 companies, a philanthropist, investor, and a business magnate.'[56]

What's his secret? He operates an open-door policy to everyone in his organisation and is willing to listen to anyone who works for him. As Derrick Diksa puts it, 'How empowering would it be to know you could go to the top of the organisation to give your opinion directly to the CEO without fear of repercussion?'[57]

Social responsibility

More and more customers and investors are looking for organisations that take their social responsibility seriously, going beyond lip service. They are asking questions about the values and ethics of the organisation and the way it treats its employees – customers know this is an excellent indication of the integrity, transparency and trustworthiness of the business.

Research has found that customers and clients are more likely to have stronger purchase intentions when an organisation demonstrates corporate social responsibility.[58] This needs to start from within, by being responsible for the well-being of your own people. Open and ethical leadership plays an enormous role in implementing ethical practices and creating a reputation for corporate social responsibility.[59]

Example: Jacinda Ardern

Let's step away from the private sector for a moment to look at a leader in the political arena. Whether or not you agree with her policies, New Zealand Prime Minister Jacinda Ardern has made headlines around the world for her leadership style, especially her compassion and vulnerability after the Christchurch terror attack on two mosques, which saw fifty-one lives lost and many injured.

In a time of pain and suffering, and with the potential for escalating violence and division of the community over the attack, Ardern broke down many barriers when she hugged victims, wearing a black headscarf as a simple show of respect. A few days later, when she addressed New Zealand's Parliament, she made a small but bold statement by opening her remarks with the Islamic greeting 'As-Salaam Alaikum' and gave a unified cry, 'They are us.'[60]

Ardern's actions and willingness to be vulnerable helped to unite communities, cultures and the whole country and demonstrated the importance of mourning together. Biographer Madeleine Chapman shared, 'Her grace and compassion following the Christchurch mosque shooting captured the world's attention. Oprah Winfrey invited us to "channel our inner Jacindas" as praise for Ardern flooded headlines and social media.'[61]

Ardern herself uses various social media platforms to connect directly to people. She has used Facebook Live to read letters and questions she has received from community members and to clarify messages from her government. During the COVID-19 pandemic, she explained details about her government's COVID response. Reaching out to real people in this way demonstrates that for Ardern, communication is a two-way street and creating connection through vulnerability is a strength. In 2021, Ardern's leadership was recognised as she topped *Fortune* magazine's world's fifty greatest leaders.[62]

Revenue

Reputation and revenue are closely interrelated. Revenue is the reward for achieving a solid reputation in the marketplace. You can also optimise profit by reducing losses from incidents like theft or costly exposure. This is important, as the financial implications of a risk incident can be considerable.

People impact profit

Creating a Safe Zone in your work environment enhances employee performance, leading to more productive teams, with flow-on effects on revenue and business resilience. People who enjoy coming to work and feel valued in the workplace engage more effectively with both their internal and external customers. Research has found that organisations can lower operational costs and increase profits by focusing on collective trust within the organisation.[63]

Employee retention also improves. A 2010 report from the World Economic Forum found that organisations that promote well-being among their workforce have higher rates of retention and higher rates of employee engagement, productivity and creativity, all of which impact the bottom line.[64]

A positive work culture can also affect your organisation's value in the stock market. A 2019 Oxford Economics study found that 'elements such as employee collaboration, engagement, retention, and client satisfaction have a tangible impact on revenue growth and stock price.'[65]

On the other side of the equation, getting it wrong is costly. Organisations are spending far more on responding to incidents in the workplace. According to the Ponemon Institute's *2020 Cost of Insider Threats: Global Report*, the activities that drive these rising costs are monitoring and surveillance, investigation, escalation, incident response, containment, ex-post analysis and remediation. The fastest growing cost centre of these is investigation, with the average cost across all incident types rising 86% in only two years to $103,798.[66]

In a disengaged workplace, issues such as low attention levels, high error rates and absenteeism – which could be related to mental health problems such as stress and anxiety – take a huge toll on revenue. The South Australian Health and Medical Research Institute (SAHMRI) has reported that workplace stress and anxiety and other mental illness causes the loss of nine million working days each year in Australia. This is equal to $190 billion annually, or 12% of GDP.[67]

There is so much evidence to support the financial and reputational benefits of looking after your people and building trust, not to mention the reduced organisational risk exposure.

CASE STUDY: The Campbell's Soup story

If you're looking for a great example of the importance of connecting with employees to support a rebuild of a corporate brand with integrity, look no further than the Campbell's Soup story. It shows how one leader, willing to stand by his convictions, completely turned a company around.

In 2001, Campbell's was struggling. Sales were on a downward slide, thanks to a decision to raise the prices of the iconic canned soup, and the company's market value had halved. Doug Conant decided to take the role of CEO at Campbell's, leaving his previous position as president of Nabisco Foods Co. Conant had a strong belief in employee engagement and he wasn't afraid to implement it, developing a ten-year plan to turn the company around.

Sensing resistance from his leadership team, Conant made sweeping and controversial changes. He replaced 300 of the company's top 350 leaders in his first few months. This made a huge statement, not only to the employees, but also to the market. It demonstrated Conant's commitment to far-reaching change. He had a motto: 'To win in the marketplace, you must first win the workplace.'[68] He understood the need to connect with people and build confidence and trust through his approach and actions.

Did his gamble pay off? It certainly did. After completing his ten-year plan, Conant retired in 2011 with an impressive record: Campbell's stock had outperformed the Standard & Poor's Index. During that time, Campbell's also won the Gallup Great Workplace Award four times and a Catalyst Award for advancing the careers of women in the workplace.

Trust is the pathway that Conant believed in. In his words, 'Trust enables you to execute with excellence and produce extraordinary results. As you execute with excellence and deliver on your commitments, trust becomes easier to inspire, creating a flywheel of performance.'[69]

Business ethics affect business performance

A high degree of corporate social responsibility can give you the edge in a competitive market. We've seen this in the wake of the Financial Services Royal Commission in Australia, which has seen bank customers flee the Big Four to smaller banks that are perceived to be more ethical. More and more customers are looking for organisations they trust will reflect their own values, especially younger markets, who are insisting on higher standards of corporate social responsibility.

Research shows the link between business ethics and business performance, and the critical role that ethical executive leadership plays in this.[70] As Kim and Brymer have observed, 'Ethical leadership behaviours are more than good behaviour, they are key to a successful operation. Through influencing these factors there is a direct positive impact on market share and competitive performance.'[71]

CASE STUDY: Microsoft

Microsoft presents an interesting case study because it has gone through stages where it has done well and when things have gone poorly. At one point, matters were reportedly going so badly that each department was working in its own silo, and the departments were actively antagonistic towards one another.

But a change in leadership – current CEO, Satya Nadella – brought the company back on course. Nadella shared a new mission with his employees: 'To empower every person and every organisation on the planet to achieve more.' He talks about engagement, purpose and the importance of meaningful work.

The *Harvard Business Review* has listed Microsoft at number five among its 'Top 20 Business Transformations of the Last Decade', saying, 'We believe it's the decision to infuse a higher purpose into the culture, one that guides strategic decisions and gives clarity to everyday tasks, that has propelled these companies to success'.[72]

It takes strong and brave leadership to embark on a journey that focuses on the power of their people. But as you will hear me say often, there is reward in the right type of effort.

Risk and leadership

There is an enormous difference between a leader and an executive. When you think of an executive, you think of the job. Executives are in an official position, charged with managing the day-to-day running of an organisation. They make decisions, implement strategies and give instructions. Executives are all about the execution.

Some people believe that once they achieve an executive role – when the word 'executive' is on their business card – they automatically become a leader via the power of their position, regardless of their actual leadership skills. A sign of a poor leader that many people have shared with me is when you speak with them, you walk away feeling like they were talking *at* you, not with you. Or if they do check in with you, it can feel disingenuous, like they were ticking the box, rather than offering genuine engagement.

There is nothing automatic about true leadership. Leadership has nothing to do with a job title, and you do not have to hold an executive role to be a leader. Leadership is the ability to inspire and motivate people, and to demonstrate the way forward.

You can recognise true leaders by their willingness to openly share their views, strategies and beliefs – they value transparency and unfiltered communication. In turn, they value and listen to the views of others. Great leaders welcome and embrace passion, creativity and the willingness to innovate. They understand the importance of inclusivity and diversity, knowing that a broad range of views and backgrounds brings a broader range of ideas and solutions.

True leaders push the envelope. They seek out great people and nurture talent, often with the desire to see other, future leaders step forward. They create opportunities for collaboration, feedback and testing, and encourage their teams to challenge one another in a positive way. In short, they create a positive environment in the workplace that is almost contagious. That culture becomes one of the most attractive features of working for the organisation.

Any organisation that can fill its executive roles with skilled leaders will see an amazing transformation in terms of employee satisfaction, workplace culture, customer service, business reputation and increased revenue. It's when you have that combination of the two – an executive leader – that you see companies transform.

Through this chapter, I have mentioned a number of strong leaders within industry and government. But leaders can come from anywhere.

Example: Greta Thunberg

At fifteen years of age, a Swedish student and environmental activist caught the world's attention when she challenged world leaders to take immediate action against climate change.

Greta Thunberg began her protest by sitting outside the Swedish parliament on school days, holding a sign that read *Skolstrejk för klimatet* ('School strike for climate').

She was soon joined by other students and began an organised school climate strike called Fridays for the Future. A few months later, she was addressing the United Nations Climate Change Conference, inspiring millions of students across the globe to join protests. Student strikes took place every week somewhere in the world.

Thunberg is a straight shooter, voicing what many are reluctant to say. She is a perfect example of a leader who is not an executive or politician, and she was not even an adult when she started. You don't need to be any of these things to be a leader, you just need to have a vision, passion, voice and a plan.[73]

Summary

Though you may set out to mitigate risk, if you implement the PROTECT framework, you'll also begin to see startlingly positive impacts on your reputation and revenue. These are the flow-on effects of focusing on people, leveraging a different perspective on risk and employing a balanced approach that looks through the lens of both risk *to* people and risk *by* people.

In this chapter, we've seen how the evidence stacks up – whether it comes from the field of business strategy, psychology or political science. If you focus on the well-being of your employees, you'll improve the reputation and revenue of your business, create a workplace where people are proud to come to work and reduce your organisational risk profile.

11
Turning Risk Into Opportunity

We've seen how the PROTECT framework can work not only to reduce risk, but also to improve reputation and increase revenue. But this model also has the power to take you from reacting to risk, to proactively managing it, then even to predicting it and preventing it.

Turning the dial from a reactive approach to risk towards positive improvements is what you are striving for. You achieve this by aligning the purpose and goals of all the people in your organisation through a strong organisational culture that focuses so clearly on the well-being of your people, that they want to reciprocate the goodwill. This is where your valued people can also become human risk sensors for your organisation and enable you to take advantage of the opportunities that go hand in hand with risk.

Human sensors

What are human sensors? Humans are social animals. When we focus on the well-being of someone, place or thing, we become protective of that person, place or thing. We naturally become aware of threats to the things that are important to us, often instinctively.

This instinctive desire people have to protect what is important can also apply to the organisation they work for. Engaged employees want to protect the well-being of the organisation and this can provide the opportunity for employees to become human sensors – proactively sensing risk, both internal and external.

Most people want to do the right thing by their organisation.[74] Unless they have a reason to disengage, the majority of people will naturally feel a level of protection for the people and organisations they work with. A team of human sensors is a team in which everyone is looking out for threats to one another and the organisation. They become monitors and signal or step in when required to ensure the organisation is protected from harm. Your people are in every corner of your business. They are communicating with customers and working intimately with every process and technology. They are often the first to notice a potential threat, and can act as your early warning system. They might raise a concern about safety issues or speak to a manager when they see a colleague struggling.

Many organisations have technological systems that use detection as part of their toolkit. They can be important to your arsenal of tools, but these systems have limitations or gaps and still rely on people for implementation, development and analysis. People can leverage their intuition and observation skills. Early detection and response from your team prevents or heavily reduces the impact of harm, not to mention the associated costs.

If your people are not engaged, they might see a potential threat and think, 'Oh, that's someone else's problem.' But if they are engaged, they are far more likely to come to you and say, 'Hey, look – I've noticed something doesn't seem quite right here. I just wanted to raise it and see what you think about it.' These conversations, sounding out areas of potential harm, are among the most effective ways to reduce organisational risk.

Activating human sensors

Implementing the PROTECT framework will help you activate your human sensors. How? Because this framework creates the fundamental conditions that inspire people to become your risk sensors. Let's start by revisiting the foundations for this – the Safe Zone.

The Safe Zone activates human sensors

A Safe Zone is critical to activating effective human sensors. Without a Safe Zone, your people will not feel safe to bring warnings and alerts to your attention. As we saw in Chapter 6, a Safe Zone is built around a culture where it's safe to succeed, and equally safe to fail. It's built on open communication where no one is going to shoot the messenger, and instead important information is passed on and acted on.

Organisations that don't operate in a Safe Zone place everyone in the workplace at increased risk. Research has found that serious risks, even loss of life, can be attributed to a failure to heed or action warnings, and this failure stems from cultural problems in the workplace.[75]

In a Safe Zone, employees are also more likely to identify their own vulnerabilities and seek support. The stigma that accompanies any admission of vulnerability in other workplaces is replaced with a supportive, compassionate, and responsive work environment. Your employees are able to seek help before they become a risk to your organisation, whether through absenteeism, disengagement, low productivity or more damaging behaviour. If you have individuals who do exhibit these behaviours, they will be the ones who stand out, especially if your culture is based around a Safe Zone and inclusiveness.

Supportive organisational culture

Once a Safe Zone has been established, a supportive organisational culture can grow. What does it feel like to work in one? A supportive culture binds the organisation together through a shared vision and common goals. Each person feels genuinely acknowledged for their contribution. When they have feedback or suggestions to share, they have the opportunity to offer them, and they feel that their voice is heard. They also feel that their own values are reflected in the demonstrated values of the organisation.

As we have seen, this benefits the company through staff retention. According to Mansor and Saufi, 'Employees who feel their personality, goals, and values align with those of the role and the organisation are more likely to stay with the organisation, rather than leaving.'[76] Research has also linked workplace cultures that value innovation with mature risk management practices.[77]

When you review the research and collateral around enterprise risk management and workplace cultures, it highlights the benefits such as a risk-focused culture, improved risk focus and awareness, and the utilisation of resources, communication, monitoring and reporting (including against regulatory and compliance obligations).

The key piece in being effective in Enterprise Risk Management (ERM) is connecting employees to the organisation, so they feel motivated to protect the company. What underpins this is usually a couple of key components:

- They connect to the company's purpose or mission and they believe they have a valued part to play.

- They are in a Safe Zone and believe the company cares about them and their well-being… and that they are valued.

It is this connection that provides the foundation to educate employees on the types of harm that can affect their work environment and the business, and how each of them is critical to the company's safety and protection. When they are motivated to care about the company's well-being, then they can become your 'risk sensors'.

Ethical leadership

Having had the privilege to have worked in and with a lot of large organisations, it's rare for me to see one in which the whole organisation is getting it right. Instead, what I find are pockets of success. Typically these teams will be headed by an inspirational leader who seems to achieve better results than others and operates with a strong ethical framework. These leaders have higher employee retention – in fact, you often find many people within the organisation want to transfer to this high-performing team. There is evidence that ethical leaders reduce employee turnover and prevent behaviours that can cause an organisation harm.[78] The team members have a connection, often with pride and a sense of protection, to both the manager and the team itself. The manager may have often already created a Safe Zone which provides the opportunity for the employees to become your human risk sensors.

Going back to the case study of Douglas Conant from Campbell's Soup, his reputation for social responsibility and ethical leadership resulted in him not only becoming an internationally renowned business leader, but a *New York Times* and *Wall Street Journal* bestselling author, a keynote speaker and social media influencer. His business success story demonstrates performance beyond the market he was working in. The result of his leadership approach not only elevated the reputation of his business brand, but of himself as an individual leader.

A clear plan

Good leaders are good planners. When it comes to risk, it's important to have a process in place, so that when something goes wrong, there is clear guidance on how to handle it: there's a process, a drill or a play-book that is purpose-built for your people.

But there must also be a plan around preventing risk. Processes and procedures must be put in place to actively monitor areas of risk and continually look for improvements. You can't leave gaping holes in areas that will expose you. This requires an informed and balanced view.

Your employees connect in every aspect of your business, so leveraging their knowledge, skills and observations to aid in identifying potential risk is crucial. There is an opportunity here to follow the touchpoints of your employees, looking at the way your people interact with every business process, every technology and every person internally and externally that they come into contact with while fulfilling their job function. Following these threads and using the Risk Lens is an excellent way to uncover risks, as well as to identify opportunities to develop innovative solutions.

Business resilience

Human sensors are one benefit of implementing the PROTECT framework. Another is business resilience. According to the Australian Department of Home Affairs, 'Organisational resilience refers to a business's ability to adapt and evolve as the global market is evolving, to respond to short-term shocks – be they natural disasters or significant changes in market dynamics – and to shape itself to respond to long-term challenges.'[79]

When you create a 'safe to succeed' environment, and employees are connected to the organisation and its well-being (ie they are human risk sensors), business resilience is a by-product. A safety culture has been shown to provide not only risk management, but also institutional resilience.[80]

Such an environment creates a workforce ecosystem of talented and committed people who will navigate risks and be motivated to work through challenges. They support the organisation because they trust the organisation to support them, plus, they are aligned to the organisational mission or values. These organisations are in turn more resilient to disruptions such as market shifts, economic shocks, and social upheaval.[81]

CASE STUDY: COVID resilience

The business community was hit hard during the COVID-19 pandemic, but there were examples of employees working collaboratively with their companies to find ways to keep the lights on and positively impact business resilience. Some employees volunteered to take leave or reduced wages through the tough time. Others cut their hours, so their peers who

---

> were supporting families could keep their jobs. The *Fiji Sun* reported that nine Pacific Destinations employees sacrificed their jobs so that others could stay in work.[82] There were also senior executives who stopped paying themselves a salary, such as Qantas CEO Alan Joyce,[83] among other international executives.[84]
>
> Companies that support their people often find support from their people, even in the face of an unexpected event like COVID-19. When times are tough, your people will rally.

Opportunity and risk come in pairs

As we have seen, the amazing thing about risk is that it always contains the seeds of opportunity. Most people deal with risk reactively, responding after a negative event to clean up the mess. But if you go deeper and start to look at vulnerabilities and threats before a negative incident occurs, you will often find opportunities to enact something more powerful, not just to put on a band-aid or tick a compliance box.

For example, many organisations must attain ISO compliance or certification under another standard. Some companies see this as a tedious duty, and work through the checklists with little joy. But others have turned these compliance responsibilities into an art form. They have developed innovative solutions to meet compliance requirements, such as through developing software, systems and protocols that are scalable and transferable to other organisations. They have built products around their compliance solutions and are able to market these services to other organisations. They have gone beyond a tick-box approach to champion their solution and show what good risk management processes can look like.

As the Department of Home Affairs has said, the idea is not to just survive or bounce back from adversity but to 'bounce forward', 'to improve aspects of the organisation's functioning so that in adversity it not only survives but possibly gains from the situation.'[85]

From reactive to proactive to preventative

In many organisations, you will find pockets that appear to be more proactive and others more reactive. But there is normally an overall business theme, a perception of risk along the spectrum of reactive to proactive. You often don't find organisations sit in the middle. Internal and external customers will sense the organisation is either proactive or reactive. Where do you think your organisation falls in the spectrum – is it reactive or proactive?

Often we can ignore problems until something happens to us and there's harm done to us in some way, physically, emotionally, psychologically or financially.

Only then do we think, 'I don't want to do that again.' We put a process in place to avoid it. This is the reactive approach.

Through the PROTECT framework, we're turning the dial from a reactive to a proactive approach and stepping into the prevention arena. Once you look at the threats and vulnerabilities and overall risk associated to people, you see possibilities and potential. You start to conduct individual risk assessments and begin to think about what's important. What are the consequences? What are the domino effects? How does this affect things up or down the chain (eg other departments, customers)?

These questions lead to more proactive thinking – anticipating events, coming up with people-focused playbooks and processes, thinking about how to protect what's important, perhaps putting in place regular reviews, accessing advice from experts or hiring new recruits with innovative ideas and skills.

As time goes on, you surround yourself with people, processes, systems and technologies that help you to look at things in a more predictive and even preventative way. You move from anticipating negative events, mitigating threats and removing obstacles to actively predicting trends and changes that have not yet posed a threat. You might begin to use a range of smart analytics. You might start to track new types of indicators and notice patterns that you haven't seen before.

CASE STUDY: Turning the dial

It is exciting when you work with teams who start turning the dial from reactive to proactive to predictive and preventative. I worked with an organisation who had a fraud alert system that was generating an overwhelming amount of noise. There were so many alerts, they simply couldn't process all the information. Their response to this noise was reactive. They had things falling through the gaps and they couldn't be sure why so many alerts were being generated. This was due to the black box system which did not specify why the alerts were being raised, which meant the client could not view the potential limitations or gaps of the system. While there was a tool in place, due to a lack of transparency, the client could not gauge the true risk to the organisation.

We worked closely with the client's team to understand how their analysts used the current systems, but also what they were really trying to achieve. The new analytical system we provided was not only able to detect the same fraud events they had already been detecting, but also discovered fraud indicators that had not been previously detected through their existing tools and processes.

This helped our client with the visibility they required, plus proactively prioritised and triaged their information, so they felt back in control. Through the signals that had not been detected previously, we uncovered infiltrators who were trying to test their system in ways that they had not previously identified. And because they'd never seen this before, they hadn't been looking for it. We set up a new alert to specifically target this developing vulnerability and signals that allowed the team to proactively analyse trends and patterns. We took the client from a typical reactive approach through a proactive triage system all the way to a predictive approach.

The Protect the House Promise

When coaching organisations about how to turn risk into reward, I offer them a promise – the Protect the House Promise. By implementing the PROTECT framework effectively, they will be turning the dial to create a powerful desire among all employees to protect their house – not just the organisation but the home of the business itself, the land, the people, the brand, the reputation and everything that sits within it.

The house may be symbolic of a whole business or a department, an agency or a home. Whatever the organisational structure, it's about uniting all the key stakeholders, everyone that resides there, to focus on protecting what is important. Whether you're a small organisation, a large multinational corporation or government agency, everything you want to protect sits under that roof. And as we have learned, risks and disruptions can be better navigated when employees are motivated to protect the house.[86]

Summary

Wherever there is risk, there is also opportunity. Leveraging our unique perspective, system and framework empowers the best efforts of your people, free of the fear of failure. It creates a 'safe to succeed' environment that builds trust and collaboration between people, teams and leadership.

In these environments, people become an organisation's best protection as they begin to act as human sensors, discovering and communicating potential risks before they affect the business. By approaching risk through a people-centred lens, you activate this powerful risk management asset: your own people. The result is the confidence to improve and manage the Three Rs – reputation, revenue and risk.

The approach also allows you to turn the risk management dial from reactive to proactive, all the way to predictive and even preventative. But the most rewarding part of the journey is seeing and feeling the difference of an engaged team of employees who are motivated to protect the well-being of the business – to protect the house.

Conclusion

The tools and strategies outlined in *Risk Starts and Ends with People* provide everything you need to create a workplace that predicts and prevents risk by activating your greatest asset: your people.

Once you put people at the centre of risk, and begin to view risk through the Risk Lens, you'll be surprised by how quickly you pick up on potential risk. You'll be more alert to the stressors acting on your employees. You'll notice the places where frustration may lead to risk. You'll identify possible risk in the chatter you hear from your employees. In short, you'll be well prepared to prevent all sorts of risk.

The PROTECT framework puts people at the centre of risk. It provides a clear Risk Lens, to enable you to see how risk operates both as risk *to* a person and risk *by* a person, and how these are inextricably linked. It also shows the origins of risk in people – their risk cocktail, which includes their predisposition and the stressors operating on them that can lead to a trigger moment and onset. The consequences of this can be devastating for everyone around them. We've seen how this system can be understood like a game of Russian Roulette, where your organisation is the potential victim of this dangerous game of chance.

But we've also seen how you can work to turn this around, by implementing the latter elements of the PROTECT framework. You can build trust and confidence in your organisation through authenticity and transparency. You can optimise your work environment by creating a Safe Zone, where employees are supported to succeed without the fear of failure. You can collaborate to 'win with' your team and your partners to fill gaps, increase knowledge and identify biases. And you can implement your intelligent toolkit, which ensures that the right tool is deployed for the job.

As we have seen, the benefits of this approach extend well beyond risk mitigation. It will positively impact on your reputation and revenue, improve your workplace culture, and increase your standing as an ethical leader. Knowing that risk starts and ends with people will help you to focus on the importance of connecting with your people, not just to reduce risk, but to harness their best efforts for your business. It's your people who touch all aspects of your business to ensure its success. When you build a 'safe to succeed environment', you unlock the potential of your people to create opportunity for your organisation.

Risk starts and ends with people. People are at the centre of all risk and your business. Only by focusing on risk with, through and by your people, are you going to truly solve your risk exposure and drive transformational change.

I encourage you to share the insights in this book with your teams. You can access further free resources on the Unearth website (www.unearth.com.au) and find out more about our services in providing people-centred solutions.

Notes

1. Walter B Cannon, 'The James-Lange theory of emotions: A critical examination and an alternative theory', *The American Journal of Psychology*, 39, 1/4 (1927), 106–124, https://doi.org/10.2307/1415404
2. C Osborne, 'Microsoft account hijack vulnerability earns bug bounty hunter $50,000', ZDNet, 3 March 2021, www.zdnet.com/article/microsoft-account-hijack-vulnerability-earns-bug-bounty-hunter-50000, accessed 8 May 2021
3. W Turton and J Robertson, 'Microsoft attack blamed on China morphs into global crisis', Bloomberg, 7 March 2021, www.bloombergquint.com/business/hackers-breach-thousands-of-microsoft-customers-around-the-world, accessed 8 May 2021
4. AS ISO 31000: 2018, *Risk Management – Guidelines*, Standards Australia Limited, 2018
5. Commonwealth of Australia, 'Royal Commission into National Natural Disaster Arrangements', 2020, https://naturaldisaster.royalcommission.gov.au/publications/html-report, accessed 9 May 2021
6. Commonwealth of Australia, *Royal Commission into Misconduct in the Banking, Superannuation and Financial*

Services Industry, 2019, www.royalcommission.gov.au/
royal-commission-misconduct-banking-superannuation-
and-financial-services-industry, accessed 9 May 2021

7. Source Global Research, *The Global Risk Services Market in
2019*, 2019, https://reports.sourceglobalresearch.com/
report/download/5055/extract/The-Global-Risk-Services-
Market-in-2019, accessed 9 May 2021

8. Allied Market Research, 'Risk management market to reach
$18.50 bn, globally, by 2026 at 14.6% CAGR: Allied Market
Research', Cision PR Newswire, 14 November 2019, www.
prnewswire.com/news-releases/risk-management-market-
to-reach-18-50-bn-globally-by-2026-at-14-6-cagr-allied-
market-research-300958400.html, accessed 9 May 2021

9. Simon Sinek, *Start With Why: How great leaders inspire
everyone to take action* (Portfolio, 2009)

10. Commonwealth of Australia, 'Royal Commission into
Aged Care Quality and Safety: Final Report: Care, Dignity
and Respect', 2021, https://agedcare.royalcommission.gov.
au/publications/final-report, accessed 9 May 2021

11. Urie Bronfenbrenner, 'Toward an experimental ecology of
human development', *American Psychologist*, 32, 7 (1977),
513–531, https://doi.org/10.1037/0003-066X.32.7.513

12. Beyond Blue, 'Keep your stress bucket from overflowing',
Beyond Blue, no date, www.beyondblue.org.au/personal-
best/pillar/wellbeing/keep-your-stress-bucket-from-
overflowing, accessed 9 May 2021

13. Nigel Phair, 'Identifying the insiders: How do we recognise
cyber threats within organisations?', ACS Information
Age, 8 October 2019, https://ia.acs.org.au/article/2019/
identifying-the-insiders.html, accessed 9 May 2021

14. Sune von Solms and Renier van Heerden, 'The
Consequences of Edward Snowden NSA Related
Information Disclosures', Conference: 10th International
Conference on Cyber Warfare and Security ICCWS, March
2015, www.researchgate.net/publication/275019554_
The_Consequences_of_Edward_Snowden_NSA_Related_
Information_Disclosures

15. The Myers & Briggs Foundation, 'MBTI basics', MBTI, no
date, www.myersbriggs.org/my-mbti-personality-type/
mbti-basics, accessed 9 May 2021

16. Disc profile, 'What is DiSC?', Disc profile, no date, www.
discprofile.com/what-is-disc, accessed 9 May 2021

17. Jim Harter, 'Dismal employee engagement is a sign of global mismanagement', Gallup, no date, www.gallup.com/workplace/231668/dismal-employee-engagement-sign-global-mismanagement.aspx, accessed 9 May 2021

18. John F Kennedy, 'Moon speech: 12 September 1962', NASA, no date, https://er.jsc.nasa.gov/seh/ricetalk.htm, accessed 9 May 2021

19. Airfocus, 'What is an Agile Framework?', Airfocus, no date, https://airfocus.com/glossary/what-is-an-agile-framework, accessed 9 May 2021

20. TechTarget, 'Fail fast', TechTarget, December 2016, https://whatis.techtarget.com/definition/fail-fast, accessed 9 May 2021

21. Arrk Group, 'Fail fast, fail often: Explained', Arrk Group, no date, www.arrkgroup.com/thought-leadership/fail-fast-fail-often-explained, accessed 9 May 2021

22. Dominic Price, 'Forget about "fail fast" – just fail well', Atlassian, 22 November 2017, www.atlassian.com/blog/inside-atlassian/forget-fail-fast-just-fail-well, accessed 9 May 2021

23. Bill Taylor, 'How Coca-Cola, Netflix, and Amazon learn from failure', Harvard Business Review, 10 Nov 2017, https://hbr.org/2017/11/how-coca-cola-netflix-and-amazon-learn-from-failure, accessed 9 May 2021

24. Mental Health Australia and KPMG, 'Investing to save: The economic benefits for Australia of investment in mental health reform', 2018, https://mhaustralia.org/sites/default/files/docs/investing_to_save_may_2018_-_kpmg_mental_health_australia.pdf, accessed 9 May 2021

25. R U OK? 'How to ask R U OK?: Simple steps that could change a life', R U OK?, no date, www.ruok.org.au/how-to-ask, accessed 9 May 2021

26. Shelley Dempsey, 'Why leaders must talk to staff on mental health', Australian Institute of Company Directors, 14 September 2020, https://aicd.companydirectors.com.au/membership/membership-update/why-leaders-must-talk-to-staff-on-mental-health?utm_source=AdobeCampaign&utm_medium=email&utm_campaign=MembershipUpdate&utm_content=DM4268900&TC=DM4268900, accessed 9 May 2021

27. The Ponemon Institute, *2020 Cost of Insider Threats: Global Report* (The Ponemon Institute, 2020)

28. Beaumont People, *Meaningful Work Insights*, Beaumont People, 2019, https://go.meaningfulwork.com.au/research, accessed 9 May 2021

29. Human Resources Director, 'What do Australians constitute as meaningful work?', Human Resources Director, 25 November 2019, www.hcamag.com/au/specialisation/workplace-health-and-safety/what-do-australians-constitute-as-meaningful-work/192956, accessed 29 March 2021

30. John Hollon, 'Survey: Successful companies have an employee-focused culture', TLNT, 20 March 2012, www.tlnt.com/survey-finds-that-successful-companies-have-an-employee-focused-culture, accessed 9 May 2021

31. Charles Feltman, *The Thin Book of Trust: An essential primer for building trust at work* (Thin Book Publishing, 2008)

32. Stephen MR Covey, *The Speed of Trust: The one thing that changes everything* (Simon & Schuster, 2006)

33. Adrian Wilkinson et al, 'Taking the pulse at work: An employment relations scorecard for Australia', *Journal of Industrial Relations*, 60, 2 (2018), 145–175, https://doi.org/10.1177/0022185617748990

34. Cindy Robbins, 'Salesforce is #1 on the FORTUNE "100 Best Companies to Work For®" list!', Salesforce, 15 February 2018, www.salesforce.com/blog/salesforce-fortune-100-best-companies-to-work-blog, accessed 9 May 2021

35. Catherine Yoshimoto and Ed Frauenheim, 'The best companies to work for are beating the market', Fortune, 27 February 2018, https://fortune.com/2018/02/27/the-best-companies-to-work-for-are-beating-the-market, accessed 9 May 2021

36. Roger Jones, 'What CEOs are afraid of', Harvard Business Review, 24 February 2015, https://hbr.org/2015/02/what-ceos-are-afraid-of, accessed 9 May 2021

37. Vala Afshar, 'Why IT as you know it is dead (and long live the citizen developer)', ZDNet, 28 March 2018, www.zdnet.com/article/why-it-as-you-know-it-is-dead, accessed 9 May 2021

38. Erika Andersen, '21 quotes from Henry Ford on business, leadership and life', Forbes, 31 May 2013, www.forbes.com/sites/erikaandersen/2013/05/31/21-quotes-from-henry-ford-on-business-leadership-and-life, accessed 9 May 2021.

39. Quoted in Everyday Interview Tips, 'How to show you can manage conflict positively', Everyday Interview Tips, no date, https://everydayinterviewtips.com/see-how-easily-you-can-show-you-manage-conflict-positively, accessed 9 May 2021.

40. Research and Markets, *Global artificial intelligence market report 2018 with forecasts to 2025 – market to reach $190.6 billion: Growth in big data is a major driver*, Cision PR Newswire, 7 May 2018, www.prnewswire.com/news-releases/global-artificial-intelligence-market-report-2018-with-forecasts-to-2025---market-to-reach-1906-billion-growth-in-big-data-is-a-major-driver-300609110.html, accessed 9 May 2021

41. Justin Fimlaid, 'The vulnerability of Artificial Intelligence', NuHarbor Security, 28 April 2020, www.nuharborsecurity.com/cyber-vulnerability-of-artificial-intelligence, accessed 9 May 2021

42. Del Aden, 'Artificial Intelligence (AI) in the context of transformation, transition, transparency & privacy', B&FT Online, 20 November 2020, https://thebftonline.com/20/11/2020/artificial-intelligence-ai-in-the-context-of-transformation-transition-transparency-privacy, accessed 9 May 2021

43. Jennifer O'Brien, 'Australia's only female GCSIO, Dr Maria Milosavljevic reveals her top priorities', CIO, 6 September 2018, www.cio.com/article/3515499/australia-s-only-female-gcsio-dr-maria-milosavljevic-reveals-her-top-priorities.html, accessed 9 May 2021.

44. Catherine Clifford, 'Bill Gates: A.I. is like nuclear energy — "both promising and dangerous"', CNBC, 26 March 2019, www.cnbc.com/2019/03/26/bill-gates-artificial-intelligence-both-promising-and-dangerous.html, accessed 9 May 2021

45. Sebastian Kettley, 'Elon Musk's AI warning: Artificial Intelligence is a "potential danger to the public"', Express, 14 Nov 2019, www.express.co.uk/news/science/1204119/Elon-Musk-AI-warning-Artificial-Intelligence-danger-Neuralink-Elon-Musk-latest, accessed 9 May 2021

46. Lucy Ingham, 'Stephen Hawking: "The rise of powerful AI will be either the best or the worst thing ever to happen to humanity"', Factor, 14 March 2018, www.factor-tech.com/feature/stephen-hawking-the-rise-of-powerful-ai-will-be-either-the-best-or-the-worst-thing-ever-to-happen-to-humanity, accessed 9 May 2021

47. Melanie Mitchell, *Artificial Intelligence: A guide for thinking humans* (Pelican, 2020)
48. Kelsey Taylor, '5 ways how AI (Artificial Intelligence) is transforming the healthcare industry', HiTechNectar, no date, www.hitechnectar.com/blogs/ways-ai-transforming-healthcare-industry, accessed 9 May 2021
49. Accenture, 'AI: Healthcare's new nervous system', Accenture, 30 July 2020, www.accenture.com/au-en/insights/health/artificial-intelligence-healthcare, accessed 9 May 2021
50. Matthew Rozsa, 'Amazon will temporarily stop selling its facial recognition software to law enforcement', Salon, 11 June 2020, www.salon.com/2020/06/11/amazon-will-temporarily-stop-selling-its-facial-recognition-software-to-law-enforcement, accessed 9 May 2021
51. BBC, 'Uber's self-driving operator charged over fatal crash', BBC, 16 September 2020, www.bbc.com/news/technology-54175359, accessed 9 May 2021
52. Jesse Damiani, 'A voice deepfake was used to scam A CEO out of $243,000', Forbes, 3 September 2019, www.forbes.com/sites/jessedamiani/2019/09/03/a-voice-deepfake-was-used-to-scam-a-ceo-out-of-243000, accessed 9 May 2021
53. Amy Kraft, 'Microsoft shuts down AI chatbot after it turned into a Nazi', CBS News, 25 March 2016, www.cbsnews.com/news/microsoft-shuts-down-ai-chatbot-after-it-turned-into-racist-nazi
54. UK Cabinet Office, 'International public sector fraud forum guidance', Gov.uk, 10 February 2020, www.gov.uk/government/publications/international-public-sector-fraud-forum-guidance, accessed 9 May 2021
55. Priyansha Mistry, 'Richard Branson: "Clients do not come first. Employees come first."', The HR Digest, 8 October 2017, www.thehrdigest.com/richard-branson-clients-do-not-come-first-employees-come-first, accessed 9 May 2021
56. Anna Domanska, 'What makes Richard Branson a great leader?', Industry Leaders, 27 January 2018, www.industryleadersmagazine.com/makes-richard-branson-great-leader, accessed 9 May 2021
57. Derrick Diksa, 'Richard Branson: A transformational and charismatic leader', PennState, 19 June 2020, https://sites.psu.edu/leadership/2020/06/19/richard-branson-a-transformational-and-charismatic-leader, accessed 9 May 2021

58. Chieh-Peng Lin et al, 'Understanding purchase intention during product-harm crises: Moderating effects of perceived corporate ability and corporate social responsibility', *Journal of Business Ethics*, 102 (2011), 455–471, https://doi.org/10.1007/s10551-011-0824-y

59. Yan Zhu et al, 'Corporate social responsibility, firm reputation, and firm performance: The role of ethical leadership', *Asia Pacific Journal of Management*, 31, 4 (2014), 925–947, https://doi.org/10.1007/s10490-013-9369-1

60. Ashitha Nagesh, 'Jacinda Ardern: "A leader with love on full display"', BBC, 21 March 2019, www.bbc.com/news/world-asia-47630129, accessed 9 May 2021

61. Madeleine Chapman, *Jacinda Ardern: A New Kind of Leader* (The History Press, 2020)

62. Fortune, 'World's 50 Greatest Leaders', *Fortune* Magazine, no date, https://fortune.com/worlds-greatest-leaders/2021/jacinda-ardern

63. Sabrina Deutsch Salamon and Sandra L Robinson, 'Trust that binds: The impact of collective felt trust on organisational performance', *Journal of Applied Psychology*, 93, 3 (2008), 593–601, https://doi.org/10.1037/0021-9010.93.3.593

64. Alistair Dornan, *The Wellness Imperative: Creating more effective organizations*, World Economic Forum, 2010, www.right.com/wps/wcm/connect/a2bd7426-4b2a-4af9-81ac-5211e83c72bb/the-wellness-imperative-creating-more-effective-organizations-world-economic-forum-in-partnership-with-right-management.pdf?MOD=AJPERES, accessed 9 May 2021

65. Grant Thornton and Oxford Economics, *Return on Culture: Proving the connection between culture and profit*, 2019, www.oxfordeconomics.com/recent-releases/return-on-culture-proving-the-connection-between-culture-and-profit, accessed 9 May 2021

66. The Ponemon Institute, *2020 Cost of Insider Threats: Global Report* (The Ponemon Institute, 2020)

67. Christina Boedker and Kar Ming Chong, 'How to measure wellbeing at work and why it matters', UNSW Business School, 16 May 2017, www.businessthink.unsw.edu.au/articles/How-to-measure-wellbeing-at-work-and-why-it-matters, accessed 9 May 2021

68. Douglas Conant, *The Blueprint: 6 practical steps to lift your leadership to new heights* (Wiley, 2020)

69. Rick Conlow, '11 mistakes managers make in the
     performance appraisal', Rick Conlow International, 11
     January 2019, https://rickconlow.com/11-mistakes-
     managers-make-performance-appraisal, accessed
     9 May 2021
70. Silke Astrid Eisenbeiss et al, 'Doing well by doing good?
     Analyzing the relationship between CEO ethical leadership
     and firm performance', *Journal of Business Ethics*, 128, 3
     (2015), 635–651, https://doi.org/10.1007/s10551-014-2124-9
71. Woo Gon Kim and Robert A Brymer, 'The effects of ethical
     leadership on manager job satisfaction, commitment,
     behavioral outcomes, and firm performance', *International
     Journal of Hospitality Management*, 30, 4 (2011), 1020–1026,
     https://doi.org/10.1016/j.ijhm.2011.03.008
72. Scott D Anthony et al, 'The top 20 business transformations
     of the last decade', Harvard Business Review, 24 September
     2019, https://hbr.org/2019/09/the-top-20-business-
     transformations-of-the-last-decade, accessed 17 Dec. 2020
73. Martin Belam and *Guardian* staff, 'Greta Thunberg:
     teenager on a global mission to "make a difference"',
     Guardian, 26 September 2019, www.theguardian.com/
     environment/2019/sep/26/greta-thunberg-teenager-on-a-
     global-mission-to-make-a-difference
74. KCY at LAW, 'Discipline in the Workplace', KCY at LAW,
     no date, www.kcyatlaw.ca/discipline-in-the-workplace,
     accessed 9 May 2021
75. E Julie Hald et al, 'Causal and corrective organisational
     culture: A systematic review of case studies of institutional
     failure', *Journal of Business Ethics* (2020), https://doi.
     org/10.1007/s10551-020-04620-3
76. Abdul Samad kakar et al, 'Does organizational reputation
     matter in Pakistan's higher education institutions? The
     mediating role of person-organization fit and person-
     vocation fit between organizational reputation and
     turnover intention', *International Review on Public and
     Nonprofit Marketing*, 1 (2021), https://doi.org/10.1007/
     s12208-020-00266-z
77. Jinhua Chen et al, 'Organisational culture and enterprise
     risk management: The Australian not-for-profit context',
     Australian Journal of Public Administration, 78, 3 (2019),
     432–448, https://doi.org/10.1111/1467-8500.12382

78. Akanksha Bedi et al, 'A meta-analytic review of ethical leadership outcomes and moderators', *Journal of Business Ethics*, 139 (2016), 517–536, https://doi.org/10.1007/s10551-015-2625-1

79. Department of Home Affairs, 'Organisational resilience', Australian Government, no date, www.organisationalresilience.gov.au, accessed 9 May 2021

80. FW Guldenmund, 'The nature of safety culture: A review of theory and research', *Safety Science*, 34, 1–3 (2000), 215–257, https://doi.org/10.1016/S0925-7535(00)00014-X

81. Karan Sonpar et al, 'Implementing new institutional logics in pioneering organizations: The burden of justifying ethical appropriateness and trustworthiness', *Journal of Business Ethics*, 90 (2009), 345–359, https://doi.org/10.1007/s10551-009-0045-9

82. Charles Chambers, 'COVID-19: Nine sacrifice employment for colleagues', Fiji Sun, 17 March 2020, https://fijisun.com.fj/2020/03/17/covid-19-nine-sacrifice-employment-for-colleagues, accessed 9 May 2021

83. Lucy Dean, 'Qantas chief rejects his own salary as coronavirus cripples airline', Yahoo! Finance, 9 March 2020, https://au.finance.yahoo.com/news/qantas-alan-joyce-cuts-salary-230301548.html?guccounter=1, accessed 9 May 2021

84. Clare Duffy, 'Why CEOs are giving up their salaries during the coronavirus crisis', CNN Business, 26 March 2020, https://edition.cnn.com/2020/03/26/investing/ceo-giving-up-pay-coronavirus/index.html, accessed 9 May 2021

85. Department of Home Affairs, 'Organisational resilience', Australian Government, no date, www.organisationalresilience.gov.au, accessed 9 May 2021

86. CA O'Reilly III et al, 'The promise and problems of organizational culture: CEO personality, culture, and firm performance', *Group & Organization Management*, 39, 6 (2014), 595–625, https://doi.org/10.1177/1059601114550713

Acknowledgements

There have been so many amazing people who influenced and supported the process of writing this book and I cannot thank you all enough.

I would like to at least try and start with the DENT team. I was able to create my own 'Safe Zone' with the DENT team to push myself personally and my business, this past year. It was inspiring to be part of the DENT community with like-minded entrepreneurs wanting to shape their businesses to solve meaningful problems, so that each of us can be a force for good and 'make a DENT in the universe'.

To Glen Carlson, thank you for support and encouragement. Glen, you asked me a question a month or so after we first met, which became my challenge, because you could see the answer was buzzing in my head. By answering that one question, everything became clear. It provided the setting of the first domino that brought all the others in line. So really, it is your question that resulted in this book. Thank you!

To Justine Bedford, who joined me on a crazy journey. You have been my rock! You also did as I had asked. You challenged me all the way through the process. So truly, thank you for listening, sharing and questioning. Your support was incredible and instrumental in getting to where we are today. Also, thank you for laughing at my quirky ways. I will always treasure our friendship.

To the Rethink Press team – I truly want to thank Monique, Alison, Lucy and the Rethink Press Production team for your support and guidance in writing my first book. I have learned so much through this process. I am sure we will do this again.

People who know me well have often commented that I am pretty tough on myself. It can be difficult for many people to understand why this is the case. It's partly because of my predisposition (my life's journey), my ethics and values, and my inner drive to challenge myself to do better and be self-aware of my own obstacles – especially as I move forward on my own path of purpose to create a safer world. I want to ensure I am using all the skills, influence and reach I have available to make a difference (that 'dent in the universe'). Why am I mentioning this? Because the people I am thanking next are the people who understand this and have been critical in supporting me to be brave and step forward.

Dr Maria Milosavljevic, Carolyn Butler-Madden and Mark Crosweller, thank you for allowing me to be so open and vulnerable in sharing my personal life story and to find my purpose and strength from it.

Bryan Ware, Iain MacKenzie and Ross Babbage, you are gentlemen and inspirational to me. Your passion and integrity to make a difference in the world is remarkable.

Each of you has played such a vital role in supporting me to step forward as who I am, to see my strengths and not feel less for all the things I am not. I am so privileged to have each of you in my life. With all my heart, thank you.

I would like to do a personal and heartfelt call-out to all those emergency responders, defence personnel, careers and volunteers in the community trying to make our communities and the world of others safer. I want to personally thank you for all that you do and all that you are. It is your commitment to others that drives me to want to find ways to protect people like you from the harm and risks associated with your service to others.

Beyond Blue, Lifeline, RESPECT and other mental health and support services, without your services and amazing teams, so many lives would be destroyed and lost. You are very much part of our emergency responders response. Thank you for your commitment to helping and saving those who are vulnerable and suffering.

To people like Brené Brown, Margaret Wheatley, Richard Branson, Simon Sinek, Stephen Covey and the many others who are brave and open enough to step forward and share their views, beliefs, insights and passions about the power of people. Each of you has shared important messages on the strength of connecting, being vulnerable and focusing on the well-being of people to help make a difference in business and in life. Like millions of other people, your words make me feel I am not alone in my thinking and approach in life, that even though we may never meet, your support and influence is there to keep me strong. Thank you.

I also want to thank all those in the risk and risk management space, from academics to businesses, who provide effective skills, knowledge and insights to help others protect themselves and the things they value most. There is a wealth of knowledge available because of your contributions.

As I close out my acknowledgements, I want to end with the ones who influence and inspire me the most.

To my beautiful family that I adore – words will never do justice to what you mean to me. Thank you for your patience and sacrifice, and for keeping me grounded.

I want to personally thank my beautiful daughter, Jasmine, who brings a tear to my eye as I write this. You are the most precious gift I have received in my life. And you are a gift to the world, but they just don't know it yet. You inspire me and challenge me in ways no one else could, and you definitely make me want to do and be better. I love you more than you know, more than words can express.

I am going to do a quick call-out to my adorable Carla, the family Cavoodle, as she has literally been by my side the whole way through writing the book, even those 2am starts when I woke up with a thought (don't judge). Ruby, our cockatiel, has also been lovely and vocal through this time. Their love and distraction became a lifeline at times when I was in the 'writing bubble'.

To my husband, John, we have been a team and shared over half our lives together. We are so different, and those differences often challenge me, but they are also where I find my personal growth. By listening (and yes, I do listen) and respecting your views, I know those differences provide opportunities to do better. Our journey together has not been one for the faint-hearted, but look how far we have come. And the best is yet to come. Thank you for sharing your life, love and support with me.

An Invitation To Connect And Share

Thank you for investing the time to read this book. My hope is that it has given you the insight and realisation that the people around you can make the biggest and best difference in your life, both inside and outside of business. By genuinely caring about each person, their well-being and safety, your own life will transform. There truly is reward in the right type of effort.

I would like to invite you to connect with me. Nothing would make me happier than to hear your story. Maybe it's the story of a battler, with a desire to find a way forward because your path feels paved with obstacles too great to overcome alone. Or perhaps you are showing your peers, your business or the world what good leadership looks like and have insights and lessons you would like to share with me. I would truly welcome both opportunities.

There may be an aspect of the book you would like to discuss with me. One of my personal mantras and favourite quotes is, 'Be brave enough to start a conversation that matters' by Margaret Wheatley. Join me and be brave – I would welcome the opportunity to listen.

Thank you.

Lisa

The Author

As founder of risk consultancy Unearth, Lisa Sisson is driven by a strong sense of purpose, to create a safer world. She believes when people feel safe, they are empowered to give their best efforts without fear of failure.

This purpose inspires her work at Unearth, her speaking and this, her first book. It offers a unique perspective within an industry that is heavily systems-driven, making her somewhat of a 'risk rebel'.

A successful career spanning three decades, from security to technology, working for global brands and niche companies, earned her a reputation for tackling the hard problems that most shy away from.

In 2013, she launched Unearth, where she works with national security, emergency services and some of Australia's largest commercial brands. Today Lisa helps leaders who feel distracted and overwhelmed by risk management through demystifying and tackling risk in their organisations.

⊕ www.unearth.com.au

in www.linkedin.com/in/lisasisson

www.ingramcontent.com/pod-product-compliance
Lightning Source LLC
Chambersburg PA
CBHW071542200326

41519CB00021BB/6578